THIRD EDITION

EXCEL
Statistics

In Honor of Arnie and Zena

1994–2009
Outside of a dog, a book is man's best friend.
Inside of a dog, it's too dark to read.
—Groucho Marx

THIRD EDITION

EXCEL
Statistics

A QUICK GUIDE

NEIL J. SALKIND
University of Kansas

Los Angeles | London | New Delhi
Singapore | Washington DC | Boston

005.54

Los Angeles | London | New Delhi
Singapore | Washington DC | Boston

FOR INFORMATION:

SAGE Publications, Inc.
2455 Teller Road
Thousand Oaks, California 91320
E-mail: order@sagepub.com

SAGE Publications Ltd.
1 Oliver's Yard
55 City Road
London EC1Y 1SP
United Kingdom

SAGE Publications India Pvt. Ltd.
B 1/I 1 Mohan Cooperative Industrial Area
Mathura Road, New Delhi 110 044
India

SAGE Publications Asia-Pacific Pte. Ltd.
3 Church Street
#10-04 Samsung Hub
Singapore 049483

Acquisitions Editor: Vicki Knight
eLearning Editor: Katie Bierach
Editorial Assistant: Yvonne McDuffee
Production Editor: Libby Larson
Copy Editor: Jim Kelly
Typesetter: C&M Digitals (P) Ltd.
Proofreader: Jen Grubba
Indexer: Terri Corry
Cover Designer: Michael Dubowe
Marketing Manager: Nicole Elliott

Copyright © 2016 by SAGE Publications, Inc.

This book includes screenshots of Microsoft Excel 2013 to illustrate the methods and procedures described in the book. Microsoft Excel is a product of the Microsoft Corporation.

Printed in the United States of America

Library of Congress Cataloging-in-Publication Data

Salkind, Neil J.
Excel statistics : a quick guide / Neil J. Salkind. — Third edition.

pages cm
Includes index.

ISBN 978-1-4833-7404-8 (pbk. : alk. paper)
1. Microsoft Excel (Computer file) 2. Social sciences—Statistical methods—Computer programs. 3. Electronic spreadsheets. I. Title.

HF5548.4.M523S263 2016
005.54—dc23   2015006463

This book is printed on acid-free paper.

15 16 17 18 19 10 9 8 7 6 5 4 3 2 1

Contents

How to Use This Book

Who *Excel Statistics: A Quick Guide* Is For

Excel Statistics: A Quick Guide is about how to use the functions (which are predefined formulas) and the Analysis ToolPak available in Excel 2013. It was written for several general audiences.

For those enrolled in introductory statistics courses, *Excel Statistics: A Quick Guide* provides experience with the world's most popular spreadsheet program and how its features can be used to answer both simple and complex questions about data. *Excel Statistics: A Quick Guide* can also serve as an ancillary text to help students understand how an application such as Excel complements the introductory study of statistics.

For those who are more familiar with statistics, perhaps students in their second course or social or behavioral scientists or business researchers, *Excel Statistics: A Quick Guide* can be used to concisely show how functions and the Analysis ToolPak tools can be used in applied situations. These users might consider *Excel Statistics: A Quick Guide* to be a reference book from which they can pick and choose the functions or tools they need to learn as they have the need.

Excel Statistics: A Quick Guide does not teach the reader how to use Excel as a spreadsheet application. It is assumed that the user of the book has some familiarity with basic computer operations (such as clicking and dragging) and has some knowledge of how to use Excel (such as how to enter and edit data and save files). Should you desire an introductory book that combines both the basics of statistics and the use of Excel (beyond what is offered here), you might want to look at Salkind's *Statistics for People Who (Think They) Hate Statistics: Excel 2013 Edition*, also published by SAGE.

How to Use *Excel Statistics: A Quick Guide*

Excel Statistics: A Quick Guide is designed in a very special way.

Each of the 40 functions in Part I covers a two-page spread. On the left-hand side of the page is text, and on the right-hand side of the page are the figures (two per QuickGuide) that illustrate the ideas introduced in the text. This design and this format allow the user to see what the use of the Excel function looks like as it is being applied. It's easy to go from the text to the illustrations and back again if necessary.

Each of the 15 Analysis ToolPak tools in Part II uses a two-page spread as well and two figures—except that sometimes one of the figures appears on the left-hand page along with the text. This is because much of the resulting output takes up a considerable amount of physical page space and simply needs more room to be fully appreciated and understood.

With the above in mind, please note the following:

- New to this edition are two tables. The first one, "What to Use When" on page xiv, provides a breakdown of functions and Analysis ToolPak options based on the questions you are asking about your data. The second table, an expanded version of the first, can be found on page xvi and uses a flowchart format to help you determine the correct function or ToolPak option to complete the analyses you need to complete.
- If you are new to formulas or functions or the Analysis ToolPak, spend some time reading the introductions to Part I and Part II on pages 1 and 89. They will quickly get you started using these Excel features.
- If you are familiar with functions and the Analysis ToolPak, start looking through the functions and tools to get an idea of what is available and how the material is organized.
- Each of the functions and tools is accompanied by an Excel file that is used as an example. These files are available in two places: the SAGE website at study.sagepub.com/salkindexcelstats3e and from the author at njs@ku.edu. Send me a note and I will send them to you immediately.
- *Excel Statistics: A Quick Guide* is as much a reference book as anything else, and you should feel free to experiment with functions and tools that serve the same general purpose (such as the CORREL function and the Correlation ToolPak tool) to determine which work best for you in which situations and use all of Excel's very powerful features. For example, much of the output you see in *Excel Statistics: A Quick Guide* has been reformatted to better fit the page and look more attractive. This can be accomplished easily through the use of built-in Excel features such as table formatting. Excel is a very flexible tool, and you can use the output you generate through functions or through the use of tools in many different ways and in many different settings.

About the Windows and Macintosh Versions

The latest Windows and Macintosh versions of Excel are identical in many ways. The screens' appearance may be just a bit different, but that is as much a function of the operating system as it is of the Excel application. There are clear (but minor) differences between the two in how you navigate around an Excel window and how you perform certain types of operations.

For example, in Windows you can copy a cell's contents by using the Ctrl+C key combination, whereas with a Mac, you use the Command (Apple)+C key combination. Anyone familiar with either operating system will understand these differences, and you can feel comfortable using either version of the program. Once you know how to use the basics of Excel, the learning curve for the other version is not very steep.

However, the two versions continue to differ in some significant ways.

As far as functions go, the Mac version uses the simple and efficient Formula Builder to construct formulas and use functions, while the Windows version uses the similar (but a bit less friendly) Insert Function tool on the Formulas tab. At the same time, a significant disadvantage of the Mac version is that there is no Analysis ToolPak. If you want to do a more advanced analysis, like the ones we illustrate in Part II of *Excel Statistics: A Quick Guide*, then download StatPlus:mac LE (free from AnalystSoft), available as this book goes to press at www.analystsoft.com/en/products/statplusmacle/. Then use StatPlus:mac LE with the Mac version of Excel 2011.

Also, every few years, Microsoft, the developer of Excel, releases a new version of Excel. Usually, these new versions offer new and additional features, and just as often, many existing features stay the same. For the most part, the functions that you see in these pages (if available in other versions) work the same way as the functions in Excel 97 through Excel 2003 and even earlier versions of Excel, such as Version 5.0/95. So, although the images in these pages and the described steps are accurate and were developed using Excel 2013 for Windows (and Excel 2011 for the Mac), you should have no concerns that these QuickGuides will not work with your version of Excel *and with future versions*. Also, with the introduction of both the Windows and Mac versions of Excel, Microsoft added some variants of formulas. However, there are corresponding functions and Analysis ToolPak tools that will work with any version, and those are the ones that we cover.

Also, Microsoft now offers a version of Excel through Office 365, which is the web-based (or cloud) version of Microsoft Office. Office 365 is subscription based and is available through the web regardless of the platform (Windows or Mac) and operating system (Windows or OS X or Linux, for example) and all the functions we illustrate in this book should work under Office 365.

No version of Excel available? Look for substituted and open-source programs such as OpenOffice (at www.openoffice.org). You may have to look for equivalent functions in name and purpose, but most functionality is available.

About the Third Edition

This edition differs from the first two editions in some significant ways (other than what was previously discussed).

First, each Excel QuickGuide is updated for the latest and greatest Excel features, and the accompanying screen shots illustrate such.

Second, Part I now contains five new functions that deal with computing averages, tests of significance, and looking at data, further enabling the reader to grasp how to organize and analyze information.

Third, there are two new tables on pages xiv and xvi that both deal with how the user can determine what function or Analysis ToolPak option best fits the type of data being analyzed and the question being asked. These tables were requested by several users, and we hope they help make the book easier to use and more useful.

Acknowledgments and Dedication

There are always many people to thank when a book comes to fruition. Let me first thank Vicki Knight, publisher at SAGE, for her editorship, guidance, patience, and willingness to talk through lots of aspects of the project. Katie Bierach, eLearning editor, and Yvonne McDuffee, editorial assistant, are to be most gratefully thanked as well. Others to thank are Libby Larson for making this book look as good as it does (even if the author had a few crazy comments), and Jim Kelly, copy editor, who helped me answer difficult questions about how to illustrate data and what's best to include. And, thanks to all the people at SAGE, who seem to care as much about their authors as what their authors write.

This book is dedicated to my loving sister.

Corrections? Ideas? Concerns? Anything—let me know. Thanks.

Neil J. Salkind
njs@ku.edu

About the Author

Neil J. Salkind received his PhD in human development from the University of Maryland and taught at the University of Kansas for 35 years, where he is now professor emeritus of educational psychology. He has written more than 125 professional papers and presentations, and he is the author of several college-level textbooks, including *Statistics for People Who (Think They) Hate Statistics* (SAGE), *Theories of Human Development* (SAGE), *Exploring Research* (Prentice Hall), and the *Encyclopedia of Measurement and Statistics* (SAGE). Other SAGE texts by Salkind can be found at www.sagepub.com. Salkind lives in Lawrence, Kansas, where he likes to print on ancient letterpress machines, read, swim with the River City Sharks, bake brownies (see the Excel version of *Statistics for People* . . . for the recipe), and poke around old things.

What to Use When

| | | I'm describing data sets. | | | I'm looking at differences between groups. | | I'm examining relationships between variables. | | I'm working with a database. | |
		I'm looking at averages and other characteristics of distributions.	*I'm looking at variability.*	*I'm looking at how data are distributed.*	**How many groups are you working with?** *One Group*	*Two or More Groups*	*I am looking at a simple relationship.*	*I am predicting one or more variables from another.*	*I am counting the frequency of certain entries.*	*I am looking for characteristics of a data set.*
Excel Functions		AVERAGE (p. 8)	STDEV.S (p. 20)	FREQUENCY (p. 28)	Z.TEST (p. 72)	F.DIST (p. 62)	COVARIANCE.S (p. 42)	INTERCEPT (p. 48)	COUNT (p. 80)	SMALL (p. 74)
		AVERAGEA (p. 10)	STDEV.P (p. 22)	NORM.DIST (p. 30)		F.TEST (p. 66)	PEARSON (p. 46)	SLOPE (p. 50)	COUNTA (p. 82)	LARGE (p. 76)
		MEDIAN (p. 12)	VAR.S (p. 24)	PERCENTILE.INC (p. 32)		CONFIDENCE.NORM (p. 64)	CORREL (p. 44)	TREND (p. 52)	COUNTBLANK (p. 84)	AVERAGEIF (p. 78)
		MODE.SNGL (p. 14)	VAR.P (p. 26)	PERCENTILE.RANK (p. 34)		T.DIST (p. 68)	RSQ (p. 56)	FORECAST (p. 54)	COUNTIF (p. 86)	
		MODE.MULT (p. 16)		QUARTILE.INC (p. 36)		T.TEST (p. 70)	CHISQ.DIST (p. 58)			
		GEOMEAN (p. 18)		RANK.AVG (p. 38)			CHISQ.TEST (p. 60)			
				STANDARDIZE (p. 40)						
Analysis ToolPak Options		Descriptive Statistics (p. 92)	Descriptive Statistics (p. 92)	Descriptive Statistics (p. 92)	z-Test: Two Sample Means (p. 102)	t-Test: Paired Two-Sample for Means (p. 104); t-Test: Two-Sample Assuming Unequal Variances (p. 106)	Correlation (p. 119)	Regression (p. 121)		

What You Want to Find Out		
Functions		Data Analysis Toolpak Options
The Average of a Group of Data		
AVERAGE		Descriptive Statistics
AVERAGEA		Moving Average
MEDIAN		Random Number Generator
MODE.SNGL		Rank and Percentile
MODE.MULT		Sampling
GEOMEAN		
AVERAGEIF		
The Variability in a Group of Data		
STDEV.S		Descriptive Statistics
STDEV.P		Histogram
VAR.S		
VAR.P		
How Data Are Distributed		
FREQUENCY		Descriptive Statistics
NORM.DIST		Histogram
How Data Compare with Each Other		
PERCENTILE.INC		
PERCENTILE.RANK		
QUARTILE.INC		
RANK.AVG		
STANDARDIZE		
Relationships Between Data		
COVARIANCE		Correlation
PEARSON		
CORREL		
RSQ		

CHISQ.DIST		
CHISQ.TEST		
	Predicting One or More Variables	
INTERCEPT		Regression
SLOPE		
TREND		
FORECAST		
	Differences Between Samples and Populations	
Z-TEST		z-Test for Two Sample Means
	Differences Between Two or More Samples	
F.DIST		t-Test: Paired Two Sample for Means
F.TEST		t-Test: Two-Sample Assuming Unequal Variances
CONFIDENCE. NORM		t-Test: Two-Sample Assuming Equal Variances
T.DIST		Anova: Single Factor
T.TEST		Anova: Two-Factor with Replication
		Anova: Two-Factor without Replication
	Characteristics of Data in a Database	
COUNT		Histogram
COUNTA		
COUNTBLANK		
COUNTIF		
SMALL		
LARGE		
AVERAGEIF		

SAGE was founded in 1965 by Sara Miller McCune to support the dissemination of usable knowledge by publishing innovative and high-quality research and teaching content. Today, we publish more than 750 journals, including those of more than 300 learned societies, more than 800 new books per year, and a growing range of library products including archives, data, case studies, reports, conference highlights, and video. SAGE remains majority-owned by our founder, and after Sara's lifetime will become owned by a charitable trust that secures our continued independence.

Los Angeles | London | New Delhi | Singapore | Washington DC | Boston

PART I

USING EXCEL FUNCTIONS

A function is a formula that is predefined to accomplish a certain task. *Excel Statistics: A Quick Guide* deals with those tasks that are statistical in nature, and in this introduction, we will show the general steps for using any Excel function.

Although there are many different types of functions (such as AVERAGE and STDEV.S) in many different categories (such as financial, logical, and engineering), most of what we will be dealing with focuses on working with numerical data and performing elementary and advanced operations—in other words, those that fall in the group of functions known as *statistical*.

Here's a Simple Example

In Figure A1.1, you can see a column of 10 numbers, with the average appearing in Cell B11. Take a look at the formula bar at the top of the figure and you will see the syntax for this function. Like this:

=AVERAGE(B1:B10)

Figure A1.1	A Simple Function That Computes the Average of a Set of Values

B11	▼		f_x	=AVERAGE(B1:B10)

◢	A	B	C	D	E	
1		2				
2		2				
3		5				
4		7				
5		5				
6		6				
7		3				
8		6				
9		5				
10		4				
11	Average	4.5				

Some general things to remember about using functions:

1. Functions always begin with an equal sign (=) as the first character entered in a cell.

2. A function can be placed in any cell. It will return the value of that function in that cell. It often makes the most sense to place the function near the data you are describing.

3. As you can see in Figure A1.1, the syntax of the function [located in the formula bar, which is =AVERAGE(B1:B10)] is not what is returned to the cell, but rather the *value* computed by the function (in this case, 4.5).

4. A function can be entered manually by typing in the syntax and the range (or ranges of cells that are to be applied), or it can be entered automatically. We'll review both methods in this introduction, but *Excel Statistics: A Quick Guide* will focus exclusively on the automatic method because it is easier and faster, and a function can always be edited manually if necessary.

The Anatomy of a Function

Let's take a quick look at what makes up a function, and then we will move on to how to enter one.

Here's the function that you saw earlier in Figure A1.1 that computes the average for a range of scores:

=AVERAGE(B1:B10)

And, here is what each element represents:

=	Tells Excel that this is a function. You want Excel to calculate a value in the cell, not put the syntax in the cell.
AVERAGE	The name of the function.
(B1:B10)	The range of cells that hold the input to the function. In the case of the AVERAGE function, these cells hold the values whose average you want to find.

Entering a Function Manually

To enter an Excel function manually (by typing an equal sign and the name of the function and the cells you want the function to act upon), you have to know two things:

1. The name of the function.

2. The syntax or structure of the function. You can see by the example we have been using that AVERAGE is the name of the function, and the syntax is

=AVERAGE(range of cells)

Some functions are simple and others are quite complex. You can find out the names of all available Excel functions, what they do, and the associated syntax through Excel Help. You can get help on any one particular function by opening up the dialog box for that function (as you will see later) and clicking the "Help on this function" link that appears in the function dialog box.

Entering a Function Automatically

This is by far the fastest and easiest method and will be the model we will use throughout *Excel Statistics: A Quick Guide*. You still have to know what function you need to use, and in this example, we use the AVERAGE function and compute the actual value.

1. Click the cell where you want the function to be placed. In the example we are using here, the cell is B11. If you are following along, be sure you click in a cell that is blank.

2. Click the Formulas tab and then click the Insert Function button (*fx*), and you will see the Insert Function dialog box, as shown in Figure A1.2.

Figure A1.2	The Insert Function Dialog Box

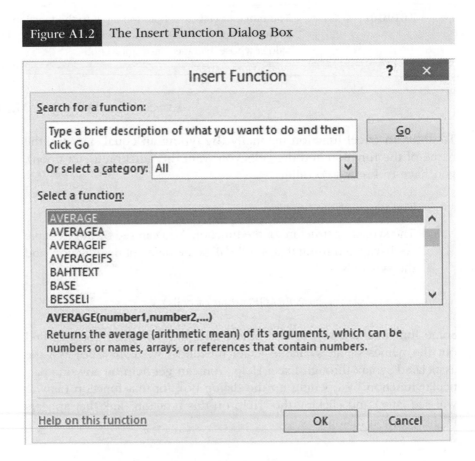

3. Locate the function you want to use by using the "Search for a function:" box and the Go button, selecting a category and a function, or selecting a function from the list that shows the most recently used functions. In our example, AVERAGE is the function of interest.

4. Double-click the AVERAGE function in the list (or any other function), and you will see the all-important Function Arguments box, shown in Figure A1.3 (with the cell addresses already completed).

Here's what's in the dialog box you see in Figure A1.3—and remember, because there is already a function in the box, you'll see cell references. If you clicked a blank cell, none would as yet have been entered.

- There's the name of the function, AVERAGE.
- Then there are text boxes, where you enter the range of cells (the argument) on which you want the function to perform its duty (B1:B10). Notice that the actual numbers (2, 2, 5, 7, 5, 6, 3, 6, 5, 4) you want to average are listed to the right of the text box.
- Right below the argument boxes is the value the function will return to the cell in which it is located (which in this case is 4.5).

Figure A1.3	The Function Arguments Dialog Box for the AVERAGE Function

Function Arguments ? ✕

AVERAGE

Number1 B1:B10 = {2;2;5;7;5;6;3;6;5;4}

Number2 = number

= 4.5

Returns the average (arithmetic mean) of its arguments, which can be numbers or names, arrays, or references that contain numbers.

Number1: number1,number2,... are 1 to 255 numeric arguments for which you want the average.

Formula result = 4.5

Help on this function   OK   Cancel

- In the middle of the dialog box (on the left) is what the function does ("Returns the average . . .").
- Next is the syntax (or directions) of how to put the function together.
- The text "Formula result = 4.5" follows.
- Finally, there is a place to get help if you need it ("Help on this function").

5. If Excel recognizes the data to which you want to apply the function, click OK and you are done. Otherwise, click the RefEdit ▦ button, and the Function Arguments box shrinks.

6. Drag the mouse over the range of cells (the data) you want included in the analysis. Click the RefEdit button.

7. Click the RefEdit button once again and then click OK. As you can see, the results are shown in the Function Arguments box and returned to the worksheet, as you see in Figure A1.1. Also note that the syntax for the function appears in the formula bar.

Another Way to Enter Functions Automatically

Another very useful way to have Excel help you insert a function is to use the Formulas tab and the More Functions option as follows.

On the Formulas tab, select More Functions → Statistical and then select the function you want to insert. You will then see whatever Function Arguments dialog box is appropriate for the function you have selected, and you can fill in the necessary information. If you intend to use the same function again, you can click the Recently Used button on the Formulas tab, and a drop-down list of functions that have been recently used (surprise) will appear.

More About Function Names

As you use the newest version of Excel, you will see that the names of the possible functions appear in the cell as you type, once you have typed an equal sign. For example, when you type =STD, you will see a drop-down box listing the STDEV.P function and the STDEV.S function, as well as several others (such as STDEVA). In this example, Excel allows you to compute several types of standard deviations. In *Excel Statistics*, we focus on those that we believe are most important, and on those that are most used. So, you will see QuickGuides for STDEV.S (QuickGuide 7) and STDEV.P (QuickGuide 8), but you will not see QuickGuides for other forms of standard deviations in this edition.

Second, certain functions are available in Excel, but they do not appear in the list of functions you see in the Insert Function dialog box. For example, RANK.AVG and RANK.EQ both appear in the Insert Function dialog box, but RANK does not. But even if it does not, it still appears when you begin to type =RAN in any cell. That's because Excel's developers want only people who have used earlier versions of Excel (where RANK was the only choice) to use that function once again, without distinguishing between RANK.AVG and RANK.EQ.

In general, we have chosen to illustrate those functions we think will best suit your needs.

More About the RefEdit Button and Collapsing and Expanding

Microsoft (the developer of Excel) thought it best to refer to the collapse and expand button as the RefEdit button. When the Function Arguments dialog box is collapsed, clicking the RefEdit button will expand the dialog box. When it is expanded, clicking the RefEdit button will collapse it. It is as simple as that.

In sum, you use the RefEdit button to collapse and expand the Function Arguments dialog box, and you are then able to drag the mouse over the cells that contain the information that the Function Arguments dialog box requires to complete the function.

EXCEL QUICKGUIDE 1

The AVERAGE Function

What the AVERAGE Function Does

The AVERAGE function takes a set of values and computes the arithmetic mean, which is the sum of the values divided by the total number of those values. It is the most often used measure of central tendency.

The Data Set

The data set used in this example is titled AVERAGE, and the question is, "What is the average speed of response and accuracy?"

Variable	Description
Response time	Speed of response across 10 items
Accuracy	Number of items correct

Using the Average Function

1. Click the cell where you want the AVERAGE function to be placed. (In the data set, the cell is B13.)

2. Select the Formulas tab and click the Insert Function button (*fx*), locate and double-click the AVERAGE function, and you will see the Function Arguments dialog box, as shown in Figure 1.1. Note that because the function is being inserted immediately below the data, Excel automatically recognizes what data should be included in the function's dialog box.

3. Click OK. The AVERAGE function returns its value in Cell B13, as you see in Figure 1.2. Copy the function to Cell C13. The average response time is 6.92, and the average accuracy is 7.60. Note that you can see the syntax for the function in the formula bar at the top of the worksheet.

Some Related Functions: MODE.MULT, MODE.SNGL, MEDIAN, GEOMEAN

Figure 1.1	The AVERAGE Function Arguments Dialog Box

Figure 1.2	The AVERAGE Function Returning the Mean Value

B13   ▾   :   × ✓ *fx*   =AVERAGE(B2:B12)

	A	B	C	D	E
1	ID	Response Time	Accuracy		
2	1	5.6	12		
3	2	7.3	3		
4	3	4.1	12		
5	4	6.8	7		
6	5	9.4	5		
7	6	10.4	2		
8	7	5.8	11		
9	8	7.8	7		
10	9	8.9	9		
11	10	3.1	8		
12					
13	AVERAGE	6.92	7.60		

Check Your Understanding

To check your understanding of the AVERAGE function, do the following two problems and check your answers in Appendix A.

QS1a. Compute the average number of Sunday afternoon museum visitors across a 12-month period. Use Data Set 1a.

QS1b. Compute the average age at which 20 undergraduates received their 4-year degrees. Use Data Set 1b.

EXCEL QUICKGUIDE 2

The AVERAGEA Function

What the AVERAGEA Function Does

The AVERAGEA function calculates the arithmetic mean of a list of values, numbers, and text.

The Data Set

The data set used in this example is titled AVERAGEA, and the question is, "What is the average age for a group of 50 seniors?" Note that age entries for some individuals (IDs #3 and #16) are missing and marked as such. AVERAGEA computes the average using the total number of entries (not just the total number of numerical values) including the number of text entries.

Variable	Description
Age	Age in years for a group of seniors

Using the AVERAGEA Function

1. Click the cell where you want the AVERAGEA function to be placed. (In the AVERAGE data set, the cell is C53.)

2. Select the Formulas tab and click the Insert Function button (*fx*), locate and double-click the AVERAGEA function, and you will see the Function Arguments dialog box, as shown in Figure 2.1.

3. Define the input range by clicking the RefEdit button and selecting the data you want to use in the analysis (in this example, Cells C2 through C51), then click the RefEdit button once again.

4. Click OK. The AVERAGEA function returns its value in Cell C53, as you see in Figure 2.2. The average age is 67.10 years. Note that you can see the syntax for the function in the formula bar at the top of the worksheet.

Some Related Functions: AVERAGE, MEDIAN, MODE.SNGL

Figure 2.1	The AVERAGEA Function Arguments Dialog Box

Figure 2.2	The AVERAGEA Function Returning the Average for the Sample

Check Your Understanding

To check your understanding of the AVERAGEA function, do the following two problems and check your answers in Appendix A.

QS2a. Compute the average score for a sample of 20 math test scores. Use Data Set 2a.

QS2b. Compute the average for the number of seniors who received shingles vaccinations in five midwestern states. Use Data Set 2b.

EXCEL QUICKGUIDE 3

The MEDIAN Function

What the MEDIAN Function Does

The MEDIAN function computes the point at which 50% of the values in a data set fall above and 50% of the values fall below. It is most often used as a measure of central tendency when there are extreme scores.

The Data Set

The data set used in this example is titled MEDIAN, and the question is, "What is the median annual income for a group of 11 homeowners?"

Variable	Description
Income	Annual income in dollars

Using the MEDIAN Function

1. Click the cell where you want the MEDIAN function to be placed. (In the data set, the cell is B14.)
2. Select the Formulas tab and click the Insert Function button (*fx*), locate and double-click the MEDIAN function, and you will see the Function Arguments dialog box, as shown in Figure 3.1. Note that because the function is being inserted immediately below the data, Excel automatically recognizes what data should be included.
3. Click OK. The MEDIAN function returns its value in Cell C13, as you see in Figure 3.2. The median income value is $56,525. Note that you can see the syntax for the function in the formula bar at the top of the worksheet.

Related Functions: AVERAGE, MODE.SNGL, GEOMEAN

Figure 3.1	The MEDIAN Function Arguments Dialog Box

Function Arguments ? ×

MEDIAN
Number1 | B2:B13 | = {35750;56525;22500;89000;43575;21...
Number2 | | = number

= 56525

Returns the median, or the number in the middle of the set of given numbers.

Number1: number1,number2,... are 1 to 255 numbers or names, arrays, or references that contain numbers for which you want the median.

Formula result = $ 113,050

Help on this function   OK   Cancel

Figure 3.2	The MEDIAN Function Returning the Median Value

B14   ▼ : × ✓ *fx* =MEDIAN(B2:B13)

	A	B	C	D	E	F
1	ID	Income				
2	1	$ 35,750				
3	2	$ 56,525				
4	3	$ 22,500				
5	4	$ 89,000				
6	5	$ 43,575				
7	6	$ 21,000				
8	7	$ 59,000				
9	8	$ 71,250				
10	9	$354,000				
11	10	$ 54,250				
12	11	$ 65,500				
13						
14	MEDIAN	$ 56,525				

Check Your Understanding

To check your understanding of the MEDIAN function, do the following two problems and check your answers in Appendix A.

QS3a. Compute the median price of a home across 10 different communities measured in dollars. Use Data Set 3a.

QS3b. Compute the median height of a group of 20 NCAA basketball players measured in inches. Use Data Set 3b.

EXCEL QUICKGUIDE 4

The MODE.SNGL Function

What the MODE.SNGL Function Does

The MODE.SNGL function computes the most frequently occurring value in a set of values.

The Data Set

The data set used in this example is titled MODE, and the question is, "What is the mode or favorite flavor of ice cream?"

Variable	Description
Preference	1 = vanilla ice cream, 2 = strawberry ice cream, 3 = chocolate ice cream

Using the MODE.SNGL Function

1. Click the cell where you want the MODE function to be placed. (In the data set, the cell is B23.)
2. Select the Formulas tab and click the Insert Function button (*fx*), locate and double-click the MODE.SNGL function, and you will see the Function Arguments dialog box, as shown in Figure 4.1.
3. Define the input range by clicking the RefEdit button and selecting the data you want to use in the analysis (in this example, Cells B2 through B21), then click the RefEdit button once again.
4. Click OK. The MODE.SNGL function returns its value in Cell B23, as you see in Figure 4.2. The mode is 3, or the preference is for chocolate ice cream. Note that you can see the syntax for the function in the formula bar at the top of the worksheet.

Related Functions: AVERAGE, MODE.MULT, GEOMEAN

| Figure 4.1 | The MODE.SNGL Function Arguments Dialog Box |

| Figure 4.2 | The MODE.SNGL Function Returning the Median Value |

Check Your Understanding

To check your understanding of the MODE.SNGL function, do the following two problems and check your answers in Appendix A.

QS4a. Compute the mode for toppings for a group of students who order ice cream sundaes. Use Data Set 4a, where 1 = hot fudge, 2 = butterscotch, and 3 = no preference.

QS4b. Compute the mode for age range of 25 respondents on a survey. Use Data Set 4b, where 1 = below 21 years, 2 = between 21 and 34 years, and 3 = over 34 years.

EXCEL QUICKGUIDE 5

The MODE.MULT Function

What the MODE.MULT Function Does

The MODE.MULT function computes the most frequently occurring values in a set of values.

The Data Set

The data set used in this example is titled MODE.MULT, and the question is, "What are the most frequently occurring item prices from 10 different stores?"

Variable	Description
Store #	The store number containing the item
Item price	The price of the item in dollars

Using the MODE.MULT Function

1. Highlight the cells where you want the MODE.MULT function to be placed. (In the data set, the cells are B22 through B25.)

2. Select the Formulas tab and click the Insert Function button (*fx*), locate and double-click the MODE.MULT function, and you will see the Function Arguments dialog box, as shown in Figure 5.1.

3. Define the input range by clicking the RefEdit button and selecting the data you want to use in the analysis (in this example, Cells B2 through B21), then click the RefEdit button once again.

4. Because the MODE.MULT function operates only on arrays of numbers, use the Ctrl+Shift+Enter keys together, and the MODE.MULT function returns its value in Cells B22 through B25, as you see in Figure 5.2. The modes are $2.53 and $2.95. Note that you can see the syntax for the function in the formula bar at the top of the worksheet, with brackets {} around the formula indicating that this is an array. The "#N/A" in Figure 5.2 indicates that additional modes could have been placed in those cells, but since there were only two modes, the other cell (B25) goes unfilled.

Related Functions: AVERAGE, MEDIAN, MODE.SNGL

| Figure 5.1 | The MODE.MULT Function Arguments Dialog Box |

| Figure 5.2 | The MODE.MULT Function Returning the Average for the Sample |

Check Your Understanding

To check your understanding of the MODE.MULT function, do the following two problems and check your answers in Appendix A.

QS5a. Compute the modes for gender, where 1 = male, 2 = female, and 3 = unspecified. Use Data Set 5a.

QS5b. Compute the modes for 50 neighborhoods, where neighborhoods are coded as 1, 2, 3, 4, or 5. Use Data Set 5b.

EXCEL QUICKGUIDE 6

The GEOMEAN Function

What the GEOMEAN Function Does

The GEOMEAN function computes the geometric mean, used to compute an average of a set of numbers that are multiplied together.

The Data Set

The data set used in this example is titled GEOMEAN, and the question is, "What is the geometric mean for percent gains in achievement over a 5-year period?"

Variable	Description
ACH	Achievement gain for Years 1 through 5

Using the GEOMEAN Function

1. Click the cell where you want the GEOMEAN function to be placed. (In the data set, the cell is B8.)

2. Select the Formulas tab and click the Insert Function button (*fx*), locate and double-click the GEOMEAN function, and you will see the Function Arguments dialog box, as shown in Figure 6.1.

3. Define the Input Range by clicking the RefEdit button and selecting the data you want to use in the analysis (in this example, Cells B2 through B6), then click the RefEdit button once again.

4. Click OK. The GEOMEAN function returns its value as 0.083, or 8.3%, in Cell B9, as you see in Figure 6.2. Note that you can see the syntax for the function in the formula bar at the top of the worksheet.

Related Functions: AVERAGE, AVERAGEA, MEDIAN

Figure 6.1	The GEOMEAN Function Arguments Dialog Box

Function Arguments   ?   ×

GEOMEAN
   Number1 | |▦| = number
   Number2 | |▦| = number

                                           =

Returns the geometric mean of an array or range of positive numeric data.

                Number1: number1,number2,... are 1 to 255 numbers or names, arrays, or references that contain numbers for which you want the mean.

Formula result =

<u>Help on this function</u>   [OK]   [Cancel]

Figure 6.2	The GEOMEAN Function Returning the Median Value

B8   ▼ ⋮   ✕ ✓ f_x =GEOMEAN(B2:B6)

	A	B	C	D	E
1	Year	ACH			
2	1	12%			
3	2	9%			
4	3	6%			
5	4	5%			
6	5	12%			
7					
8	GEOMEAN	8.3%			

Check Your Understanding

To check your understanding of the GEOMEAN function, do the following two problems and check your answers in Appendix A.

QS6a. Compute the geometric mean for average achievement score for a group of 10 high schools. Use Data Set 6a.

QS6b. Compute the geometric mean for average monthly amount spent on groceries per week in dollars over a year. Use Data Set 6b.

EXCEL QUICKGUIDE 7

The STDEV.S Function

What the STDEV.S Function Does

The STDEV.S function takes a sample set of values and computes the standard deviation.

The Data Set

The data set used in this example is titled STDEV.S, and the question is, "What is the standard deviation for age for a sample of 20 sixth graders?"

Variable	Description
Age	Age in months for a group of sixth graders

Using the STDEV.S Function

1. Click the cell where you want the STDEV.S function to be placed. (In the data set, the cell is B23.)

2. Select the Formulas tab and click the Insert Function button (*fx*), and locate and double-click the STDEV.S function, and you will see the Function Arguments dialog box, as shown in Figure 7.1.

3. Define the input range by clicking the RefEdit button and selecting the data you want to use in the analysis (in this example, Cells B2 through B21), then click the RefEdit button once again.

4. Click OK. The STDEV.S function returns its value in Cell B23, as you see in Figure 7.2. The standard deviation for the sample's age is 4.99 years. Note that you can see the syntax for the function in the formula bar at the top of the worksheet.

Related Functions: STDEV.P, VAR.S, VAR.P

| Figure 7.1 | The STDEV Function Arguments Dialog Box |

| Figure 7.2 | The STDEV Function Returning the Standard Deviation for the Sample |

Check Your Understanding

To check your understanding of the STDEV.S function, do the following two problems and check your answers in Appendix A.

QS7a. Compute the standard deviation for a sample of 10 spelling test scores in percentage correct. Use Data Set 7a.

QS7b. Compute the standard deviation for the number of adults who received flu shots across five different Midwest counties. Use Data Set 7b.

EXCEL QUICKGUIDE 8

The STDEV.P Function

What the STDEV.P Function Does

The STDEV.P function computes the standard deviation for scores from an entire population.

The Data Set

The data set used in this example is titled STDEV.P, and the question is, "What is the standard deviation for the number of friendships lasting more than 1 year for a population of 90 10th graders?"

Variable	Description
Number of friends	Number of friendships lasting more than 1 year for a group of adolescents

Using the STDEV.P Function

1. Click the cell where you want the STDEV.P function to be placed. (In the data set, the cell is B8.)

2. Select the Formulas tab and click the Insert Function button (*fx*), locate and double-click the STDEV.P function, and you will see the Function Arguments dialog box, as shown in Figure 8.1.

3. Define the input range by clicking the RefEdit button and selecting the data you want to use in the analysis (in this example, Cells B2 through G16), then click the RefEdit button once again.

4. Click OK. The STDEV.P function returns its value in Cell B18, as you see in Figure 8.2. The standard deviation for the population is 1.93. Note that you can see the syntax for the function in the formula bar at the top of the worksheet.

Related Functions: STDEV.S, VAR.S, VAR.P

Figure 8.1	The STDEV.P Function Arguments Dialog Box

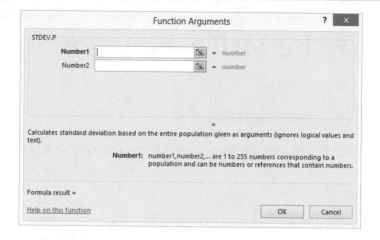

Figure 8.2	The STDEV.P Function Returning the Standard Deviation for the Population

B18   =STDEV.P(B2:G16)

	A	B	C	D	E	F	G
7		6	1	4	4	2	3
8		1	4	1	1	2	2
9		2	4	1	3	1	5
10		6	3	0	1	6	2
11		1	1	1	0	5	0
12		5	1	5	6	2	2
13		3	1	0	1	5	5
14		2	0	1	2	0	2
15		5	1	6	6	4	3
16		1	5	6	3	1	1
17							
18	STDEV.P	1.93					

Check Your Understanding

To check your understanding of the STDEV.P function, do the following two problems and check your answers in Appendix A.

QS8a. Compute the standard deviation for the population of community center monthly users. Use Data Set 8a.

QS8b. Compute the standard deviation for total sales per day at Hobbs toy store during 1 spring week. Use Data Set 8b.

EXCEL QUICKGUIDE 9

The VAR.S Function

What the VAR.S Function Does

The VAR.S function computes the variance for a set of sample scores.

The Data Set

The data set used in this example is titled VAR, and the question is, "What is the variance for the scores on The Extroversion Scale (TES) for a sample of 20 high school seniors?"

Variable	Description
TES	Score on The Extroversion Scale, ranging from 1 to 100

Using the VAR.S Function

1. Click the cell where you want the VAR.S function to be placed. (In the data set, the cell is B23.)

2. Select the Formulas tab and click the Insert Function button (*fx*), locate and double-click the VAR.S function, and you will see the Function Arguments dialog box, as shown in Figure 9.1.

3. Define the input range by clicking the RefEdit button and selecting the data you want to use in the analysis (in this example, Cells B2 through B21), then click the RefEdit button once again.

4. Click OK. The VAR.S function returns its value in Cell C13, as you see in Figure 9.2. The variance from the TES score is 246.37. Note that you can see the syntax for the function in the formula bar at the top of the worksheet.

Related Functions: STDEV.S, STDEV.P, VAR.P

Figure 9.1	The VAR.S Function Arguments Dialog Box

Figure 9.2	The VAR.S Function Returning the Variance for the Sample

Check Your Understanding

To check your understanding of the VAR.S function, do the following two problems and check your answers in Appendix A.

QS9a. Compute the variance for a sample of 20 scores on a mathematics test ranging from 1 to 100. Use Data Set 9a.

QS9b. Compute the variance for a sample of 15 scores that measure aggressive behavior ranging in value from 1 to 10. Use Data Set 9b.

EXCEL QUICKGUIDE 10

The VAR.P Function

What the VAR.P Function Does

The VAR.P function computes the variance for an entire population.

The Data Set

The data set used in this example is titled VAR.P, and the question is, "What is the variance for the scores on The Extroversion Scale (TES) for the entire population of 100 high school seniors?"

Variable	Description
TES	Score on The Extroversion Scale, ranging from 1 to 100

Using the VAR.P Function

1. Click the cell where you want the VAR.P function to be placed. (In the data set, the cell is B23.)

2. Select the Formulas tab and click the Insert Function button (*fx*), locate and double-click the VAR.P function, and you will see the Function Arguments dialog box, as shown in Figure 10.1.

3. Define the input range by clicking the RefEdit button and selecting the data you want to use in the analysis (in this example, Cells A2 through E21), and clicking the RefEdit button once again.

4. Click OK. The VAR.P function returns its value in Cell B23, as you see in Figure 10.2. The variance is 684.12. Note that you can see the syntax for the function in the formula bar at the top of the worksheet.

Related Functions: STDEV.S, STDEV.P, VAR.S

Figure 10.1 The VAR.P Function Arguments Dialog Box

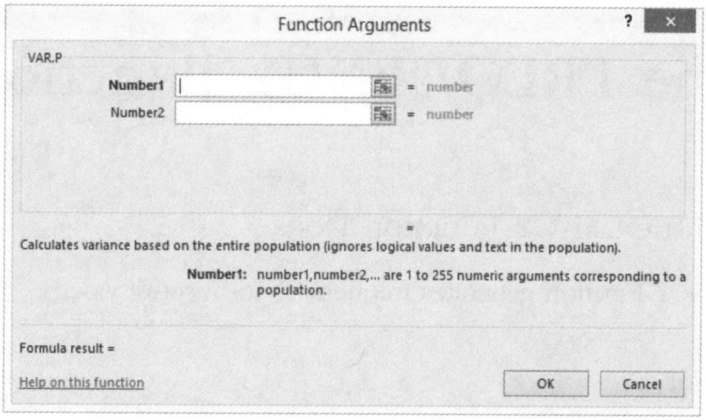

Figure 10.2 The VAR.P Function Returning the Variance for the Population

B23 =VAR.P(A2:E21)

	A	B	C	D	E
10	82	29	92	99	90
11	58	6	57	18	62
12	75	74	32	23	93
13	69	65	83	29	97
14	78	5	35	86	39
15	37	49	24	64	99
16	69	84	33	71	68
17	77	62	7	95	47
18	89	71	58	39	59
19	65	95	54	11	57
20	76	18	97	47	58
21	90	42	52	49	29
22					
23	VAR.P	684.12			

Check Your Understanding

To check your understanding of the VAR.P function, do the following two problems and check your answers in Appendix A.

QS10a. Compute the variance for the population of annual income for all bread-winners in a county of 25 cities. Use Data Set 10a.

QS10b. Compute the variance for the population of body mass index values for all 100 students in an entire elementary school. Use Data Set 10b.

EXCEL QUICKGUIDE 11

The FREQUENCY Function

What the FREQUENCY Function Does

The FREQUENCY function generates frequencies for a set of values.

The Data Set

The data set used in this example is titled FREQUENCY, and the question is, "What is the frequency of level of preference for TOOTS, a new type of cereal, by 50 consumers?"

Variable	Description
Preference	Preference on a scale from 1 through 5

Using the FREQUENCY Function

1. Create the bins (1, 2, 3, 4, and 5) into which you want the frequencies counted (as shown in Cells I2 through I6 in the FREQUENCY data set).

2. Highlight all the cells (J2 through J6) where you want the frequencies to appear.

3. Select the Formulas tab and click the Insert Function button (*fx*), locate and double-click the FREQUENCY function, and you will see the Function Arguments dialog box, as shown in Figure 11.1.

4. Click the RefEdit button in the Data_array entry box and drag the mouse over the range of cells you want included in the analysis (B2 through G11). Click the RefEdit button.

5. Click the RefEdit button in the Bins_array entry box and drag the mouse over the range of cells that defines the bins (I2 through I6). Click the RefEdit button.

6. Press the Ctrl+Shift+Enter keys in combination (not in a sequence). This is done because Excel treats Cells J2 through J6 as an array, not as a single value. In Figure 11.2, you can see the result of the function, with frequencies listed beside the values in the bin. Note in the formula bar that the function is bounded by brackets, {}, indicating that the values are part of an array.

Related Functions: NORM.DIST, PERCENTILE.INC, PERCENTRANK.INC, QUARTILE.INC, RANK.AVG, STANDARDIZE

Figure 11.1	The FREQUENCY Function Arguments Dialog Box

Figure 11.2	The FREQUENCY Function Returning the Frequencies of Values

J2 · : × ✓ f_x {=FREQUENCY(B2:G11,I2:I6)}

	A	B	C	D	E	F	G	H	I	J
1		Preference							Bins	FREQUENCY
2		2	1	1	1	3	5		1	10
3		2	2	4	5	4	1		2	14
4		2	3	5	2	1	3		3	11
5		5	2	3	1	4	2		4	8
6		3	2	5	5	5	3		5	17
7		4	4	1	1	5	5			
8		1	4	2	3	2	3			
9		5	3	4	4	2	2			
10		5	2	5	5	5	1			
11		2	5	5	3	5	3			

Check Your Understanding

To check your understanding of the FREQUENCY function, do the following two problems and check your answers in Appendix A.

QS11a. Generate a frequency histogram for the classes of 100 patients according to the following status code: 1 = ambulatory, 2 = nonambulatory. Use Data Set 11a.

QS11b. Generate a frequency histogram for the classes of 250 hotel guests according to the following rating-of-service code: 1 = loved the service, 2 = didn't like the service, 3 = couldn't care less. Use Data Set 11b.

EXCEL QUICKGUIDE 12

The NORM.DIST Function

What the NORM.DIST Function Does

The NORM.DIST function computes the cumulative probability of a score.

The Data Set

The data set used in this example is titled NORM.DIST, and the question is, "What is the cumulative probability associated with a spelling test score of 9?"

Variable	Description
Spelling score	Number of words spelled correctly out of 20

Using the NORM.DIST Function

1. Click the cell where you want the NORM.DIST function to be placed. (In the data set, the cell is C2.)
2. Select the Formulas tab and click the Insert Function button (*fx*), locate and double-click the NORM.DIST function, and you will see the Function Arguments dialog box, as shown in Figure 12.1.
3. For the X entry box, click the RefEdit button and enter the location of the value for which you want to compute the probability (in the data set, it is Cell B2).
4. For the Mean and Standard_dev entry boxes, click the RefEdit button and enter the appropriate cell addresses (B14 for Mean and B15 for Standard_dev). Note that you need to have these values already computed before you can use this function.
5. For the Cumulative entry box, type "True."
6. Click OK, and the cumulative probability will be computed in Cell C2. In this example, the cumulative probability associated with a spelling score of 9 is .07, or 7%.
7. Edit the function in Cell C2 to include absolute references for Cells B14 and B15, as you see in Figure 12.2. Copy this result from Cells C3 through C12, and the results of the probabilities associated with scores of 9 through 19 will appear, as shown in Figure 12.2.

Related Functions: FREQUENCY, PERCENTILE.INC, PERCENTRANK.INC, QUARTILE.INC, RANK.AVG, STANDARDIZE

Figure 12.1	The NORM.DIST Function Arguments Dialog Box

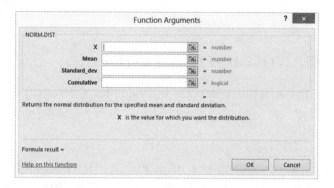

Figure 12.2	The NORM.DIST Function Returning the Cumulative Probability for a Set of Spelling Scores

C2   ▼   :   ×   ✓   *fx*   =NORM.DIST(B2,$B$14,$B$15,TRUE)

	A	B	C	D	E
1		Spelling Score	NORM.DIST (Cumulative Probability)		
2		9	7%		
3		10	11%		
4		11	18%		
5		12	27%		
6		13	38%		
7		14	50%		
8		15	62%		
9		16	73%		
10		17	82%		
11		18	89%		
12		19	93%		
13					
14	Class Mean	14			
15	Class sd	3.32			

Check Your Understanding

To check your understanding of the NORM.DIST function, do the following two problems and check your answers in Appendix A.

QS12a. Compute the cumulative probabilities for sales by month. Use Data Set 12a.

QS12b. Compute the cumulative probabilities for number of cars in a dealer's inventory by quarter. Use Data Set 12b.

EXCEL QUICKGUIDE 13

The PERCENTILE.INC Function

What the PERCENTILE.INC Function Does

The PERCENTILE.INC function computes the value for a defined percentile.

The Data Set

The data set used in this example is titled PERCENTILE.INC, and the question is, "What are the percentile values for strength in a sample of twenty-five 55-year-olds?"

Variable	Description
Strength	Amount of weight lifted

Using the PERCENTILE.INC Function

1. Click the cell where you want the PERCENTILE.INC function to be placed. (In the data set, the cell is D1.)

2. Select the Formulas tab and click the Insert Function button (*fx*), locate and double-click the PERCENTILE.INC function, and you will see the Function Arguments dialog box, as shown in Figure 13.1.

3. Click the RefEdit button in the Array entry box and drag the mouse over the range of cells (B2 through B26) you want included in the analysis. Click the RefEdit button.

4. Click the RefEdit button in the K entry box and click the cell (C2) for which you want to compute the percentile value.

5. Click the RefEdit button and press the return key or click OK. The PERCENTILE.INC function returns its value as 171 in Cell D2. The percentile values were then copied from Cells D2 through D11, as you see in Figure 13.2, paying attention to the array being edited as relative references ($B$2, etc.). Note that you can see the syntax for the function in the formula bar at the top of the worksheet.

Related Functions: FREQUENCY, NORM.DIST, PERCENTRANK, QUARTILE.INC, RANK.AVG, STANDARDIZE

Figure 13.1	The PERCENTILE.INC Function Arguments Dialog Box

Figure 13.2	The PERCENTILE.INC Function Returning the Standard Deviation

	A	B	C	D	E	F	G
1	ID	Strength	Percentile	PERCENTILE.INC (Value)			
2	1	149	100%	171.0			
3	2	142	90%	157.6			
4	3	117	80%	149.6			
5	4	132	70%	147.0			
6	5	152	60%	145.4			
7	6	171	50%	134.0			
8	7	134	40%	128.2			
9	8	166	30%	122.2			
10	9	101	20%	119.4			
11	10	147	10%	109.4			

Check Your Understanding

To check your understanding of the PERCENTILE.INC function, do the following two problems and check your answers in Appendix A.

QS13a. In the set of data for use of library facilities by weekday for the entire month of June, what is the value of the 50th percentile? Use Data Set 13a.

QS13b. In the set of data for the number of meals prepared by month for the entire year, what is the value of the 80th percentile? Use Data Set 13b.

EXCEL QUICKGUIDE 14

The PERCENTRANK.INC Function

What the PERCENTRANK.INC Function Does

The PERCENTRANK.INC function computes the percentage rank of a particular value in a data set.

The Data Set

The data set used in this example is titled PERCENTRANK.INC, and the question is, "What is the percentile rank (or percentile) for the individual who lifts 149 pounds?"

Variable	Description
Strength	Amount of weight lifted

Using the PERCENTRANK.INC Function

1. Click the cell where you want the PERCENTRANK.INC function to be placed. (In the data set, the cell is C2.)

2. Select the Formulas tab and click the Insert Function button (*fx*), locate and double-click the PERCENTRANK.INC function, and you will see the Function Arguments dialog box, as shown in Figure 14.1.

3. Click the RefEdit button in the Array entry box.

4. Drag the mouse over the range of cells (B2 through B26) you want included in the analysis and click the RefEdit button.

5. Click the RefEdit button in the X entry box.

6. Click the X value (Cell B2) for which you want to compute the PERCENTRANK. INC or percentile rank.

7. Click OK. The PERCENTRANK.INC function returns its value as 79% in Cell C2. The percentile values were then copied from Cells C2 through C26, as you see in Figure 14.2, paying attention to the array being edited as relative references ($C$2, etc.). Note that you can see the syntax for the function in the formula bar at the top of the worksheet.

Related Functions: FREQUENCY, NORM.DIST, PERCENTILE.INC, QUARTILE.INC, RANK.AVG, STANDARDIZE

Figure 14.1	The PERCENTRANK.INC Function Arguments Dialog Box

Figure 14.2	The PERCENTRANK.INC Function Returning the Percentile Rank for the Set of Scores

C2 — =PERCENTRANK.INC($B$2:$B$26,B2)

	A	B	C
1	ID	Strength	PERCENTRANK.INC (Value)
2	1	149	79%
3	2	142	54%
4	3	117	17%
5	4	132	46%
6	5	152	83%
7	6	171	100%
8	7	134	50%
9	8	166	96%
10	9	101	4%
11	10	147	67%

Check Your Understanding

To check your understanding of the PERCENTRANK.INC function, do the following two problems and check your answers in Appendix A.

QS14a. Compute the value of the percentage rank for a test score of 89. Use Data Set 14a.

QS14b. Compute the value of the percentage rank for a house sale value of $156,500. Use Data Set 14b.

EXCEL QUICKGUIDE 15

The QUARTILE.INC Function

What the QUARTILE.INC Function Does

The QUARTILE.INC function computes the values that divide a set of data into quartiles or fourths.

The Data Set

The data set used in this example is titled QUARTILE.INC, and the question is, "What is the first quartile (or 25th percentile) in a set of health scores for a group of 25 nonsmokers?"

Variable	Description
Health score	Risk for chronic illness score from 1 to 50

Using the QUARTILE.INC Function

1. Click the cell where you want the QUARTILE.INC function to be placed. (In the data set, the cell is D2.)

2. Select the Formulas tab and click the Insert Function button (*fx*), locate and double-click the QUARTILE.INC function, and you will see the Function Arguments dialog box, as shown in Figure 15.1.

3. Click the RefEdit button in the Array entry box.

4. Drag the mouse over the range of cells (B2 through B26) you want included in the analysis and click the RefEdit button.

5. Click the RefEdit button in the Quart entry box and click the RefEdit button.

6. Click in the Quart value you want to compute (Cell C2) to compute the first quartile.

7. Click OK. The QUARTILE.INC function returns its value as 27 in Cell D2, as you can see in Figure 15.2. The second, third, and fourth quartiles were computed as well. Note that you can see the syntax for the function in the formula bar at the top of the worksheet.

Related Functions: FREQUENCY, NORM.DIST, PERCENTILE.INC, PERCENTRANK. INC, RANK, STANDARDIZE

Figure 15.1	The QUARTILE.INC Function Arguments Dialog Box

Figure 15.2	The QUARTILE.INC Function Returning the Quartile for a Set of Scores

Check Your Understanding

To check your understanding of the QUARTILE.INC function, do the following two problems and check your answers in Appendix A.

QS15a. Compute the value of the second quartile for a listing of 25 spelling test scores with 20 items. Use Data Set 15a.

QS15b. Compute the third quartile for a set of health care costs at 20 area hospital emergency rooms. Use Data Set 15b.

EXCEL QUICKGUIDE 16

The RANK.AVG Function

What the RANK.AVG Function Does

The RANK.AVG function computes the percentage rank of a particular value in a data set.

The Data Set

The data set used in this example is titled RANK.AVG, and the question is, "What is the relative rank for a set of 20 grade point averages?"

Variable	Description
GPA	Grade point average

Using the RANK.AVG Function

1. Click the cell where you want the RANK.AVG function to be placed. (In the data set, the cell is C2.)

2. Select the Formulas tab and click the Insert Function button (*fx*), locate and double-click the RANK.AVG function, and you will see the Function Arguments dialog box, as shown in Figure 16.1.

3. Click the RefEdit button in the Number entry box and click the value for which you want to compute the rank (Cell B2).

4. Click the RefEdit button in the Ref entry box and drag the mouse over the array of values being ranked (B2 through B21).

5. Click the RefEdit button and press the Enter key or click OK. The RANK.AVG function returns its value as 5 in Cell C2 (for a GPA of 3.4), as you see in Figure 16.2. The ranks for all the other data points were computed as well. When ranks are copied, absolute references need to be used for the cell range B2 through B21 (appearing as $B$2:$B$21). Note that you can see the syntax for the function in the formula bar at the top of the worksheet.

Related Functions: FREQUENCY, NORM.DIST, PERCENTILE.INC, PERCENTRANK. INC, QUARTILE.INC, STANDARDIZE

| Figure 16.1 | The RANK.AVG Function Arguments Dialog Box |

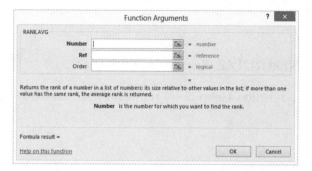

| Figure 16.2 | The RANK.AVG Function Returning the Rank for a Set of Scores |

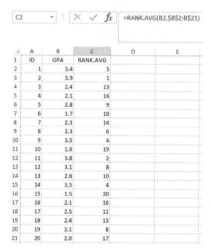

Check Your Understanding

To check your understanding of the RANK.AVG function, do the following two problems and check your answers in Appendix A.

QS16a. Compute the ranking for a score of 57 from a set of 50 response times as measured in seconds. Use Data Set 16a.

QS16b. Compute the ranking for Team 6 of 25 teams for total points scored in a season. Use Data Set 16b.

EXCEL QUICKGUIDE 17

The STANDARDIZE Function

What the STANDARDIZE Function Does

The STANDARDIZE function computes a normalized or standard score.

The Data Set

The data set used in this example is titled STANDARDIZE, and the question is, "What are the normalized scores for a set of raw test scores on the INT, a measure of introversion?"

Variable	Description
INT	A measure of introversion ranging from 1 to 25

Using the STANDARDIZE Function

1. Click the cell where you want the STANDARDIZE function to be placed. (In the data set, the cell is C2.)

2. Select the Formulas tab and click the Insert Function button (*fx*), locate and double-click the STANDARDIZE function, and you will see the Function Arguments dialog box, as shown in Figure 17.1.

3. Click the RefEdit button in the X entry box and click the value for which you want to compute STANDARDIZE (Cell B2). Click the RefEdit button.

4. Click the RefEdit button in the Mean entry box and click the mean of the values being standardized (Cell B23). Click the RefEdit button.

5. Click the RefEdit button in the Standard_dev entry box and click the STDEV of the values being standardized (Cell B24). Click the RefEdit button.

6. Click the RefEdit button and press the Enter key or click OK. The STANDARDIZE function returns its value as –0.58 in Cell C2, as you can see in Figure 17.2, and the standardized scores for all the other data points were also computed (using relative references for the mean and standard deviation). The syntax for the function in the formula bar is shown at the top of the worksheet.

Related Functions: FREQUENCY, NORM.DIST, PERCENTILE.INC, PERCENTRANK. INC, QUARTILE.INC, RANK.AVG

Figure 17.1	The STANDARDIZE Function Arguments Dialog Box

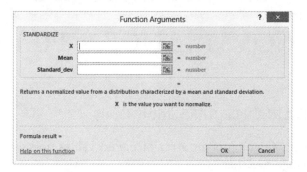

Figure 17.2	The STANDARDIZE Function Returning Standardized Values for a Set of Scores

C2 =STANDARDIZE(B2,$B$23,$B$24)

	A	B	C	D
1	ID	INT	STANDARDIZE	
2	1	12	-0.58	
3	2	15	-0.08	
4	3	14	-0.24	
5	4	21	0.93	
6	5	23	1.26	
7	6	25	1.59	
8	7	7	-1.41	
9	8	15	-0.08	
10	9	21	0.93	
11	10	8	-1.24	
12	11	22	1.09	
13	12	15	-0.08	
14	13	14	-0.24	
15	14	22	1.09	
16	15	19	0.59	
17	16	17	0.26	
18	17	9	-1.08	
19	18	10	-0.91	
20	19	3	-2.08	
21	20	17	0.26	
22				
23	AVERAGE	15.45		
24	STDEV.S	6.00		

Check Your Understanding

To check your understanding of the STANDARDIZE function, do the following two problems and check your answers in Appendix A.

QS17a. Compute all the standardized scores for a sample of 25 test scores from a history class for the fall semester. Note that you have to compute the mean and standard deviation. Use Data Set 17a.

QS17b. Compute the standardized score for a raw score of 76 from a sample of 25 test scores from a history class for the spring semester. Use Data Set 17b.

EXCEL QUICKGUIDE 18

The COVARIANCE.S Function

What the COVARIANCE.S Function Does

The COVARIANCE.S function takes a set of paired values and estimates how much two variables change together.

The Data Set

The data set used in this example is titled COVARIANCE.S, and the question is, "What is the relationship between level of intervention and number of injuries in college athletes?"

Variable	Description
Intervention	Hours of training
Injuries	Number of injuries

Using the COVARIANCE.S Function

1. Click the cell where you want the COVARIANCE.S function to be placed. (In the data set, the cell is C23.)

2. Select the Formulas tab and click the Insert Function button (*fx*), locate and double-click the COVARIANCE.S function, and you will see the Function Arguments dialog box, as shown in Figure 18.1.

3. Click the RefEdit button in the Array1 entry box and drag the mouse over the range of cells (B2 through B21) you want included in the analysis. Click the RefEdit button.

4. Repeat Step 3 for Array2 (Cells C2 through C21), and click the RefEdit button and press the Enter key or click OK. The COVARIANCE.S function returns its value as –1.9053 in Cell C23, as you see in Figure 18.2. You can see the syntax for the function in the formula bar at the top of the worksheet.

Related Functions: CORREL, PEARSON, INTERCEPT, SLOPE, TREND, FORECAST, RSQ

Figure 18.1	The COVARIANCE.S Function Arguments Dialog Box

Function Arguments ? ×

COVARIANCE.S

Array1 [ ] 🔢 = array

Array2 [ ] 🔢 = array

=

Returns sample covariance, the average of the products of deviations for each data point pair in two data sets.

Array1 is the first cell range of integers and must be numbers, arrays, or references that contain numbers.

Formula result =

Help on this function [OK] [Cancel]

Figure 18.2	The COVARIANCE.S Function Returning the Function's Value

C23 fx =COVARIANCE.S(B2:B21,C2:C21)

	A	B	C	D	E	F
1	ID	Intervention	Injuries			
2	1	6	4			
3	2	7	5			
4	3	5	6			
5	4	8	7			
6	5	7	6			
7	6	7	8			
8	7	6	6			
9	8	5	5			
10	9	6	4			
11	10	7	8			
12	11	8	7			
13	12	8	7			
14	13	9	1			
15	14	8	3			
16	15	7	2			
17	16	6	4			
18	17	4	8			
19	18	3	7			
20	19	2	9			
21	20	5	9			
22						
23	COVARIANCE.S		-1.9053			

Check Your Understanding

To check your understanding of the COVARIANCE.S function, do the following two problems and check your answers in Appendix A.

QS18a. Compute the covariance for time to first response and correct responses for 15 sixth graders. Use Data Set 18a.

QS18b. Compute the covariance for a set of hours of weekly study time and grade point average (GPA) for 25 college 1st-year students. Use Data Set 18b.

EXCEL QUICKGUIDE 19

The CORREL Function

What the CORREL Function Does

The CORREL function computes the value of the Pearson product–moment correlation between two variables.

The Data Set

The data set used in this example is titled CORREL, and the question is, "What is the correlation between height and weight for 20 sixth graders?"

Variable	Description
Height	Height in inches
Weight	Weight in pounds

Using the CORREL Function

1. Click the cell where you want the CORREL function to be placed. (In the data set, the cell is C23.)

2. Select the Formulas tab and click the Insert Function button (*fx*), locate and double-click the CORREL function, and you will see the Function Arguments dialog box, as shown in Figure 19.1.

3. Click the RefEdit button in the Array1 entry box and drag the mouse over the range of cells (B2 through B21) you want included in the analysis. Click the RefEdit button.

4. Repeat Step 3 for Array2 (Cells C2 through C21), and then click the RefEdit button and click OK. The CORREL function returns its value as 0.7759 in Cell C23, as you see in Figure 19.2. You can see the syntax for the function in the formula bar at the top of the worksheet.

Related Functions: COVARIANCE.S, PEARSON, INTERCEPT, SLOPE, TREND, FORECAST, RSQ

Figure 19.1	The CORREL Function Arguments Dialog Box

Figure 19.2	The CORREL Function Returning the Correlation

C23   ▾ : × ✓ *fx*   =CORREL(B2:B21,C2:C21)

	A	B	C	D	E	F
1	ID	Height	Weight			
2	1	60	134			
3	2	63	143			
4	3	71	156			
5	4	58	121			
6	5	61	131			
7	6	59	117			
8	7	64	125			
9	8	67	126			
10	9	63	143			
11	10	52	98			
12	11	61	154			
13	12	58	125			
14	13	54	109			
15	14	61	117			
16	15	64	126			
17	16	63	154			
18	17	49	98			
19	18	59	143			
20	19	69	144			
21	20	71	156			
22						
23	CORREL		0.77592			

Check Your Understanding

To check your understanding of the CORREL function, do the following two problems and check your answers in Appendix A.

QS19a. Compute the correlation coefficient for number of children retained in 20 classrooms with parent's level of school involvement as measured on a scale from 1 to 10, with 10 being most involved. Use Data Set 19a.

QS19b. Compute the correlation coefficient for number of water treatment plants and incidence of infectious diseases as measured by how many of 100 residents in 10 communities. Use Data Set 19b.

EXCEL QUICKGUIDE 20

The PEARSON Function

What the PEARSON Function Does

The PEARSON function computes the value of the Pearson product–moment correlation between two variables.

The Data Set

The data set used in this example is titled PEARSON, and the question is, "What is the correlation between income and level of education for 20 households?"

Variable	Description
Income	Annual income in dollars
Level of Education	Years of education

Using the PEARSON Function

1. Click the cell where you want the PEARSON function to be placed. (In the data set, the cell is C23.)

2. Select the Formulas tab and click the Insert Function button (*fx*), locate and double-click the PEARSON function, and you will see the Function Arguments dialog box, as shown in Figure 20.1.

3. Click the RefEdit button in the Array1 entry box and drag the mouse over the range of cells (B2 through B21) you want included in the analysis. Click the RefEdit button.

4. Repeat Step 3 for Array2 (Cells C2 through C21), and then click the RefEdit button and click OK. The PEARSON function returns its value as 0.76 in Cell C23, as you see in Figure 20.2. You can see the syntax for the function in the formula bar at the top of the worksheet.

Related Functions: COVARIANCE.S, CORREL, INTERCEPT, SLOPE, TREND, FORECAST, RSQ

| Figure 20.1 | The PEARSON Function Arguments Dialog Box |

| Figure 20.2 | The PEARSON Function Returning the Correlation |

Check Your Understanding

To check your understanding of the PEARSON function, do the following two problems and check your answers in Appendix A.

QS20a. Compute the Pearson coefficient value between years in teaching and teaching evaluations from high school students for 10 classrooms as measured from 1 to 25, with 25 being a terrific teacher. Use Data Set 20a.

QS20b. Compute the Pearson coefficient between consumption of ice cream per capita in gallons and crime rate as measured by the CR scale from 1 to 10, with 10 being high crime for 15 communities. Use Data Set 20b.

EXCEL QUICKGUIDE 21

The INTERCEPT Function

What the INTERCEPT Function Does

The INTERCEPT function computes the intercept value, the point at which the regression line crosses the y-axis.

The Data Set

The data set used in this example is titled INTERCEPT, and the question is, "What is the intercept for the regression line for wins predicted by injuries for 15 teams?"

Variable	Description
Wins (Y)	Number of wins last season
Injuries (X)	Average number of weekly injuries

Using the INTERCEPT Function

1. Click the cell where you want the INTERCEPT function to be placed. (In the data set, the cell is C18.)

2. Select the Formulas tab and click the Insert Function button (fx), locate and double-click the INTERCEPT function, and you will see the Function Arguments dialog box, as shown in Figure 21.1.

3. Click the RefEdit button in the Known_y's entry box and drag the mouse over the range of cells (C2 through C16) you want included in the analysis. Click the RefEdit button.

4. Repeat Step 3 for Known_x's (Cells C2 through C16), and then click the RefEdit button and click OK. The INTERCEPT function returns its value as 4.52 in Cell C13, as you see in Figure 21.2. You can see the syntax for the function in the formula bar at the top of the worksheet.

Related Functions: COVARIANCE.S, CORREL, PEARSON, SLOPE, TREND, FORECAST, RSQ

Figure 21.1	The INTERCEPT Function Arguments Dialog Box

Figure 21.2	The INTERCEPT Function Returning the Value of the Intercept

Check Your Understanding

To check your understanding of the INTERCEPT function, do the following two problems and check your answers in Appendix A.

QS21a. Compute the intercept for the regression line predicting future income from GPA for 20 accounting students. Use Data Set 21a.

QS21b. Compute the intercept for the regression line predicting success (on a scale of 1 to 10, with 10 being most successful) from years of experience. Use Data Set 21b.

EXCEL QUICKGUIDE 22

The SLOPE Function

What the SLOPE Function Does

The SLOPE function computes the slope of the regression line.

The Data Set

The data set used in this example is titled SLOPE, and the question is, "What is the slope of the regression line that predicts wins from injuries?"

Variable	Description
Wins (Y)	Number of wins last season
Injuries (X)	Average number of weekly injuries

Using the SLOPE Function

1. Click the cell where you want the value of the SLOPE function to be returned. (In the data set, the cell is C18.)

2. Select the Formulas tab and click the Insert Function button (fx), locate and double-click the SLOPE function, and you will see the Function Arguments dialog box, as shown in Figure 22.1.

3. Click the RefEdit button in the Known_y's entry box and drag the mouse over the range of cells (C2 through C16) you want included in the analysis. Click the RefEdit button.

4. Repeat Step 3 for Known_x's (Cells B2 through B16), and then click the RefEdit button and click OK. The SLOPE function returns its value as 0.25 in Cell C18, as you see in Figure 22.2. You can see the syntax for the function in the formula bar at the top of the worksheet.

Related Functions: COVARIANCE.S, CORREL, PEARSON, INTERCEPT, TREND, FORECAST, RSQ

| Figure 22.1 | The SLOPE Function Arguments Dialog Box |

Function Arguments

SLOPE

Known_y's [   ] 📇 = array
Known_x's [   ] 📇 = array

=

Returns the slope of the linear regression line through the given data points.

Known_y's is an array or cell range of numeric dependent data points and can be numbers or names, arrays, or references that contain numbers.

Formula result =

Help on this function   OK   Cancel

| Figure 22.2 | The SLOPE Function Returning the Slope of the Regression Line |

C18   fx =SLOPE(C2:C16,B2:B16)

	A	B	C	D	E	F
1	Team ID	Injuries (X)	Wins (Y)			
2	1	8	9			
3	2	7	9			
4	3	9	6			
5	4	8	7			
6	5	7	6			
7	6	4	8			
8	7	8	9			
9	8	11	3			
10	9	5	2			
11	10	2	4			
12	11	14	10			
13	12	7	4			
14	13	6	2			
15	14	4	9			
16	15	9	7			
17						
18	SLOPE		0.25			

Check Your Understanding

To check your understanding of the SLOPE function, do the following two problems and check your answers in Appendix A.

QS22a. Compute the slope for the regression line predicting future income from GPA for 20 accounting students. Use Data Set 20a.

QS22b. Compute the slope for the regression line predicting success (on a scale of 1 to 10, with 10 being most successful) from years of experience for 10 employees. Use Data Set 22b.

EXCEL QUICKGUIDE 23

The TREND Function

What the TREND Function Does

The TREND function uses the regression line values to predict outcomes.

The Data Set

The data set used in this example is titled TREND, and the question is, "What is the predicted level of wins given injuries for members of 15 volleyball teams?"

Variable	Description
Injuries (X)	Average number of player injuries
Wins (Y)	Season wins

Using the TREND Function

1. Highlight the cells where you want the array of TREND values to appear. (In the data set, the cells are E2 through E4.)

2. Select the Formulas tab and click the Insert Function button (*fx*), locate and double-click the TREND function, and you will see the Function Arguments dialog box, as shown in Figure 23.1.

3. Click the RefEdit button in the Known_y's entry box and drag the mouse over the range of cells (C2 through C16) you want included in the analysis. Click the RefEdit button.

4. Click the RefEdit button in the Known_x's entry box and drag the mouse over the range of cells (B2 through B16) you want included in the analysis. Click the RefEdit button.

5. Click the RefEdit button in the New_x's entry box and drag the mouse over the range of cells (D2 through D4) you want included in the analysis. Click the RefEdit button.

6. Because this is an array, use the Ctrl+Shift+Enter key combination to produce the TREND function and three predicted scores of 5.27, 4.77, and 7.02, as you see in Figure 23.2. You can see the syntax for the function in the formula bar at the top of the worksheet.

Related Functions: COVARIANCE.S, CORREL, PEARSON, INTERCEPT, SLOPE, FORECAST, RSQ

Figure 23.1	The TREND Function Arguments Dialog Box

Figure 23.2	The TREND Function Returning the Predicted Scores

	A	B	C	D	E
1	Team ID	Injuries (X)	Wins (Y)	New Injuries	TREND
2	1	8	9	3	5.27
3	2	7	9	1	4.77
4	3	9	6	10	7.02
5	4	8	7		
6	5	7	6		
7	6	4	8		
8	7	8	9		
9	8	11	3		
10	9	5	2		
11	10	2	4		
12	11	14	10		
13	12	7	4		
14	13	6	2		
15	14	4	9		
16	15	9	7		

Check Your Understanding

To check your understanding of the TREND function, do the following two problems and check your answers in Appendix A.

QS23a. Compute the trend for new income scores. Use Data Set 23a.

QS23b. Compute the trend for new success scores. Use Data Set 23b.

EXCEL QUICKGUIDE 24

The FORECAST Function

What the FORECAST Function Does

The FORECAST function computes a predicted value for known values of X.

The Data Set

The data set used in this example is titled FORECAST, and the question is, "What is the predicted GPA for nine newly ranked high school students?"

Variable	Description
GPA (Y)	Grade point average
Rank (X)	High school rank (from 1 to 5)

Using the FORECAST Function

1. Highlight the cells where you want the array of FORECAST values to appear. (In the data set, the cells are E2 through E10.)

2. Select the Formulas tab and click the Insert Function button (*fx*), locate and double-click the FORECAST function, and you will see the Function Arguments dialog box, as shown in Figure 24.1.

3. Click the RefEdit button in the X entry box and drag the mouse over the range of cells (D2 through D10) you are using to predict the value of Y. Click the RefEdit button.

4. Click the RefEdit button in the Known_y's entry box and drag the mouse over the range of cells (B2 through B26) you want included in the analysis. Click the RefEdit button.

5. Click the RefEdit button in the Known_x's entry box and drag the mouse over the range of cells (C2 through C26) you want included in the analysis. Click the RefEdit button.

6. Because this is an array, use the Ctrl+Shift+Enter key combination to produce the FORECAST function and the forecast scores of 3.68, 3.32, and so on, as you see in Figure 24.2. You can see the syntax for the function in the formula bar at the top of the worksheet.

Related Functions: COVARIANCE.S, CORREL, PEARSON, INTERCEPT, SLOPE, TREND, RSQ

| Figure 24.1 | The FORECAST Function Arguments Dialog Box |

| Figure 24.2 | The FORECAST Function Returning the Forecast of the Regression Line |

E2 · : × ✓ *fx* {=FORECAST(D2:D10,B2:B26,C2:C26)}

	A	B	C	D	E	F	G
1	ID	GPA (Y)	RANK (X)	New Rank	FORECAST		
2	1	4.0	5	5	3.68		
3	2	3.2	4	4	3.32		
4	3	3.9	5	5	3.68		
5	4	2.7	3	3	2.97		
6	5	3.6	5	4	3.32		
7	6	1.9	1	5	3.68		
8	7	2.4	2	6	4.04		
9	8	3.6	4	5	3.68		
10	9	3.7	4	4	3.32		
11	10	3.2	2				

Check Your Understanding

To check your understanding of the FORECAST function, do the following two problems and check your answers in Appendix A.

QS24a. Forecast the number of new losses from the previous 10 years of win-loss data for a large Eastern university football team. Use Data Set 24a.

QS24b. Forecast new American history test scores from previous world history test scores. Use Data Set 24b.

EXCEL QUICKGUIDE 25

The RSQ Function

What the RSQ Function Does

The RSQ function computes the square of the product–moment correlation between two variables.

The Data Set

The data set used in this example is titled RSQ, and the question is, "What is the RSQ, or the amount of variance accounted for, in the relationship between income and level of education?"

Variable	Description
Income (X)	Annual income in dollars
Level of education (Y)	Years of education as a percentile

Using the RSQ Function

1. Click the cell where you want the RSQ function to be placed. (In the data set, the cell is C23.)

2. Select the Formulas tab and click the Insert Function button (*fx*), locate and double-click the RSQ function, and you will see the Function Arguments dialog box, as shown in Figure 25.1.

3. Click the RefEdit button in the Known_y's entry box and drag the mouse over the range of cells (C2 through C21) you want included in the analysis. Click the RefEdit button.

4. Repeat Step 3 for the Known_x's entry box (Cells C2 through C21), and then click the RefEdit button and click OK. The RSQ function returns its value as 0.58 in Cell C23, as you see in Figure 25.2. You can see the syntax for the function in the formula bar at the top of the worksheet.

Related Functions: COVARIANCE.S, CORREL, PEARSON, INTERCEPT, SLOPE, TREND, FORECAST

| Figure 25.1 | The RSQ Function Arguments Dialog Box |

Function Arguments

RSQ

Known_y's [ ] = array
Known_x's [ ] = array

=

Returns the square of the Pearson product moment correlation coefficient through the given data points.

Known_y's is an array or range of data points and can be numbers or names, arrays, or references that contain numbers.

Formula result =

Help on this function

OK   Cancel

| Figure 25.2 | The RSQ Function Returning the Squared Correlation |

C23   ▾ : ✕ ✓ *fx*   =RSQ(C2:C21,B2:B21)

	A	B	C	D	E
9	8	$ 30,445	3		
10	9	$ 35,052	2		
11	10	$ 35,976	4		
12	11	$ 57,250	10		
13	12	$ 37,526	4		
14	13	$ 39,274	2		
15	14	$ 55,613	9		
16	15	$ 46,775	7		
17	16	$ 30,552	5		
18	17	$ 51,331	9		
19	18	$ 54,391	8		
20	19	$ 36,178	1		
21	20	$ 41,616	2		
22					
23	RSQ		0.577117757		

Check Your Understanding

To check your understanding of the RSQ function, do the following two problems and check your answers in Appendix A.

QS25a. Compute the squared correlation between height in inches and weight gain in pounds for 20 male 1st-year college students. Use Data Set 25a.

QS25b. Compute the squared correlation between quality of health care (from 1 to 5, with 5 being most healthy) and decline in infant mortality (deaths per 1,000 live-born infants) for five communities. Use Data Set 25b.

EXCEL QUICKGUIDE 26

The CHISQ.DIST Function

What the CHISQ.DIST Function Does

The CHISQ.DIST function computes the probability of a value associated with a chi-square (χ^2) value. Use the CHISQ.DIST function for computing the χ^2 value.

The Data Set

The data set is titled CHISQ.DIST and consists of the following variables. The question being asked is, "What is the probability of a Type I error or alpha level associated with a chi-square value of .29?"

Variable	Value
Chi-square value	Value of chi-square
Degrees of freedom	Degrees of freedom associated with the original chi-square analysis

Using the CHISQ.DIST Function

1. Click the cell where you want the CHISQ.DIST function to be placed. (In the data set, the cell is B4.)

2. Select the Formulas tab and click the Insert Function button (*fx*), locate and double-click the CHISQ.DIST function, and you will see the Function Arguments dialog box, as shown in Figure 26.1.

3. Click the RefEdit button in the X entry box and enter the chi-square value. In this example, it is Cell B1. Click the RefEdit button.

4. Click the RefEdit button in the Deg_Freedom entry box and click on the cell (B2) indicating the degrees of freedom.

5. Click the RefEdit button and enter "True" for the Cumulative value.

6. Click OK, and the CHISQ.DIST function returns its value of 0.13 in Cell B4, as you see in Figure 26.2, indicating that it is highly likely that this value occurred by chance. Note that you can see the syntax for the function in the formula bar at the top of the worksheet.

Related Functions: CHISQ.TEST

Figure 26.1	The CHISQ.DIST Function Arguments Dialog Box

Figure 26.2	The CHISQ.DIST Function Returning the Probability Associated With a Chi-Square Value

Check Your Understanding

To check your understanding of the CHISQ.DIST function, do the following two problems and check your answers in Appendix A.

QS26a. Compute the CHISQ.DIST value for a chi-square value of 7.8 with 10 degrees of freedom. Use Data Set 26a.

QS26b. Compute the CHISQ.DIST value for a chi-square value of 11.5 with 23 degrees of freedom. Use Data Set 26b.

EXCEL QUICKGUIDE 27

The CHISQ.TEST Function

What the CHISQ.TEST Function Does

The CHISQ.TEST function computes the probability of the chi-square (χ^2) value for a test of independence for a nominal or categorical variable.

The Data Set

The data set used in this example is titled CHISQ.TEST, and the question is, "Are the actual and expected values for party affiliation independent of one another?"

Variable	Description
Party affiliation	Frequency of actual and expected values for Democratic, Republican, and independent voters

Using the CHISQ.TEST Function

1. Click the cell where you want the CHISQ.TEST function to be placed. (In the data set, the cell is B10.)

2. Select the Formulas tab and click the Insert Function button (*fx*), locate and double-click the CHISQ.TEST function, and you will see the Function Arguments dialog box, as shown in Figure 27.1.

3. Click the RefEdit button in the Actual_range entry box and drag the mouse over the range of cells (B8 through D8) you want included in the analysis. Click the RefEdit button.

4. Click the RefEdit button in the Expected_range entry box and drag the mouse over the range of cells (B4 through D4) you want included in the analysis.

5. Click the RefEdit button or press the return key and then click OK. The CHISQ.TEST function returns its value of 0.29 in Cell B10, as you see in Figure 27.2. Note that you can see the syntax for the function in the formula bar at the top of the worksheet.

Related Functions: CHISQ.DIST

Figure 27.1	The CHISQ.TEST Function Arguments Dialog Box

Figure 27.2	The CHISQ.TEST Function Returning the Chi-Square (chi2) Value

B10   ▾ : ✕ ✓ *fx*   =CHISQ.TEST(B8:D8,B4:D4)

⊿	A	B	C	D	E	F
1	Party Affiliation					
2			Expected			
3		Democratic	Republican	Independent		Total
4		80	80	80		240
5						
6			Actual			
7		Democratic	Republican	Independent		
8		70	80	90		240
9						
10	CHISQ.TEST	0.29				

Check Your Understanding

To check your understanding of the CHISQ.TEST function, do the following two problems and check your answers in Appendix A.

QS27a. Compute the probability of the chi-square value for groups of expected users of a community center. Use Data Set 27a.

QS27b. Compute the probability of the chi-square value for groups of four brand users of different detergents. Use Data Set 27b.

EXCEL QUICKGUIDE 28

The F.DIST Function

What the F.DIST Function Does

The F.DIST function computes the probability of a value associated with an *F* value. Use the F.TEST function for computing the *F* value.

The Data Set

The data set is titled F.DIST and consists of the following variables. The question being asked is, "What is the probability of a Type I error or alpha level associated with an *F* value of 1.79 with 2 and 35 degrees of freedom?"

Variable	Value
F	Value of *F*
Degrees of freedom (numerator)	Degrees of freedom associated with the numerator
Degrees of freedom (denominator)	Degrees of freedom associated with the denominator

Using the F.DIST Function

1. Click the cell where you want the F.DIST function to be placed. (In the data set, the cell is B5.)

2. Select the Formulas tab and click the Insert Function button (*fx*), locate and double-click the F.DIST function, and you will see the Function Arguments dialog box, as shown in Figure 28.1.

3. Click the RefEdit button in the X entry box, enter the *F* value (Cell B1), and click the RefEdit button.

4. Click the RefEdit button in the Deg_freedom1 entry box and enter the degrees of freedom associated with the numerator (Cell B2). Click the RefEdit button.

5. Click the RefEdit button in the Deg_freedom2 entry box and enter the degrees of freedom associated with the denominator (Cell B3). Click the RefEdit button.

6. Enter "True" in the Cumulative entry box. Click the RefEdit button and click OK. The F.DIST function returns its value of 0.82 in Cell B5, as you see in Figure 28.2, indicating that the *F* value is significant beyond the .05 level. Note that you can see the syntax for the function in the formula bar at the top of the worksheet.

Related Functions: F.TEST, T.DIST, T.TEST, Z.TEST

Figure 28.1	The F.DIST Function Arguments Dialog Box

Figure 28.2	The F.DIST Function Returning the Probability Associated With an *F* Value

Check Your Understanding

To check your understanding of the F.DIST function, do the following two problems and check your answers in Appendix A.

QS28a. Compute the F.DIST value for the data shown in Data Set 28a.

QS28b. Compute the F.DIST value for the data shown in Data Set 28b.

EXCEL QUICKGUIDE 29

The CONFIDENCE.NORM Function

What the CONFIDENCE.NORM Function Does

The CONFIDENCE.NORM function computes the confidence interval for a specific population mean.

The Data Set

The data set is titled CONFIDENCE.NORM and consists of the following variables. The question being asked is, "What is the confidence interval for a population mean of 87.5 on a test of memory recall?"

Variable	Value
Alpha or significance level	Significance level for the confidence interval
Standard deviation (STDEV.P)	Population standard deviation
Size	Population size

Using the CONFIDENCE.NORM Function

1. Click the cell where you want the CONFIDENCE.NORM function to be placed. (In the data set, the cell is C56.)

2. Select the Formulas tab and click the Insert Function button (*fx*), locate and double-click the F.DIST function, and you will see the Function Arguments dialog box, as shown in Figure 29.1.

3. Click the RefEdit button in the Alpha entry box, enter the alpha value (Cell C53), and click the RefEdit button.

4. Click the RefEdit button in the Standard_dev entry box and enter the cell address containing the population standard deviation (Cell C54). Click the RefEdit button.

5. Click the RefEdit button in the Size entry box and enter the cell address containing the population size (Cell C55).

6. Click the RefEdit button and click OK. The CONFIDENCE.NORM function returns its value of 3.48 in Cell C56, as you see in Figure 29.2, indicating that range of expected values at the .05 level of confidence is the average score 79 ± 3.48, or (75.52 to 82.48).

Related Functions: F.TEST, T.DIST, T.TEST, Z.TEST

Figure 29.1	The CONFIDENCE.NORM Function Arguments Dialog Box

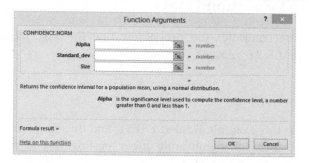

Figure 29.2	The CONFIDENCE.NORM Function Returning the Confidence Interval for a Specific Population Mean

C56 =CONFIDENCE.NORM(C53,C54,50)

	A	B	C	D	E	F
43		42	98			
44		43	73			
45		44	62			
46		45	76			
47		46	71			
48		47	99			
49		48	95			
50		49	69			
51		50	80			
52						
53	Alpha		0.05			
54	STDEV.P		12.57			
55	Size		50.00			
56	CONFIDENCE.NORM		3.483226			

Check Your Understanding

To check your understanding of the F.DIST function, do the following two problems and check your answers in Appendix A.

QS29a. Compute the CONFIDENCE.NORM value at the .01 level of significance for number of voters in 20 counties. Use Data Set 29a.

QS29b. Compute the CONFIDENCE.NORM value at the .05 level of significance for math test scores for 25 fifth graders. Use Data Set 29b.

EXCEL QUICKGUIDE 30

The F.TEST Function

What the F.TEST Function Does

The F.TEST function computes the probability that the associated F value is not significantly different from zero.

The Data Set

The data set used in this example is titled F.TEST, and the question is, "Does using an electronically based textbook significantly affect the final test scores of two different groups of 1st-year college students?"

Variable	Description
iPod	Final test score with the e-book
No iPod	Final test score using a print book

Using the F.TEST Function

1. Click the cell where you want the F.TEST function to return its value. (In the data set, the cell is C23.)

2. Select the Formulas tab and click the Insert Function button (*fx*), locate and double-click the F.TEST function, and you will see the Function Arguments dialog box, as shown in Figure 30.1.

3. Click the RefEdit button in the Array1 entry box.

4. Drag the mouse over the range of cells (B2 through B21) you want included in the analysis and click the RefEdit button.

5. Click the RefEdit button in the Array2 entry box.

6. Drag the mouse over the range of cells (C2 through C21) you want included in the analysis and click the RefEdit button.

7. Click the RefEdit button and click OK. The F.TEST function returns its value of 0.12 in Cell C23, as you see in Figure 30.2, indicating that the difference between

the groups on final test score is not significant at the .05 level. Note that you can see the syntax for the function in the formula bar at the top of the worksheet.

Related Functions: F.DIST, T.DIST, T.TEST, Z.TEST

Figure 30.1	The F.TEST Function Arguments Dialog Box

Figure 30.2	The F.TEST Function Returning the Probability of the *F* Value

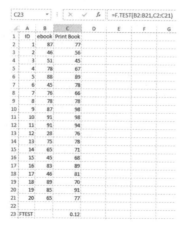

Check Your Understanding

To check your understanding of the F.TEST function, do the following two problems and check your answers in Appendix A.

QS30a. Compute the F.TEST value for the difference between attitudes (from 1 to 5, with 5 being most positive) toward using supplemental material or not on ease of completing calculation tasks. Use Data Set 30a.

QS30b. Compute the F.TEST value for the difference between two groups of calculus test scores for two different samples of 10 college juniors. Use Data Set 30b.

EXCEL QUICKGUIDE 31

The T.DIST Function

What the T.DIST Function Does

The T.DIST function computes the probability of a value associated with the Student's *t* value. Use the T.TEST function for computing the *t* value.

The Data Set

The data set is titled T.DIST and consists of the following variables. The question being asked is, "What is the probability of a Type I error or alpha level associated with a one-tailed test and a *t* value of 1.96 with 50 degrees of freedom?"

Variable	Value
X	Value of *t*
Degrees of freedom	Degrees of freedom
Tails	1 = one-tailed test, 2 = two-tailed test

Using the T.DIST Function

1. Click the cell where you want the T.DIST function to be placed. (In the data set, the cell is B5.)

2. Select the Formulas tab and click the Insert Function button (*fx*), locate and double-click the T.DIST function, and you will see the Function Arguments dialog box, as shown in Figure 31.1.

3. Click the RefEdit button in the X entry box and enter the *t* value. In this example, it is Cell B1. Click the RefEdit button.

4. Repeat Step 3 for the Deg_freedom entry box, and enter the degrees of freedom value (Cell B2), enter "True" in the Cumulative entry box, and click OK. The T.DIST function returns its value of 0.972 in Cell B5, as you see in

Figure 31.2, indicating that the *t* value is significant beyond the .05 level. Note that you can see the syntax for the function in the formula bar at the top of the worksheet.

Related Functions: F.DIST, F.TEST, T.TEST, Z.TEST

Figure 31.1	The T.DIST Function Arguments Dialog Box

Figure 31.2	The T.DIST Function Returning the Probability Associated With a *t* Value

Check Your Understanding

To check your understanding of the T.DIST function, do the following two problems and check your answers in Appendix A.

QS31a. Compute the T.DIST value for the data shown in Data Set 31a.

QS31b. Compute the T.DIST value for the data shown in Data Set 31b.

EXCEL QUICKGUIDE 32

The T.TEST Function

What the T.TEST Function Does

The T.TEST function computes the probability of the associated Student's *t* value.

The Data Set

The data set used in this example is titled T.TEST, and the question is, "Is there a significant difference in achievement scores between fall and spring tests for the same group of college students?"

Variable	Description
Fall	Fall test scores
Spring	Spring test scores

Using the T.TEST Function

1. Click the cell where you want the T.TEST function to return its value. (In the data set, the cell is C23.)
2. Select the Formulas tab and click the Insert Function button (*fx*), locate and double-click the T.TEST function. and you will see the Function Arguments dialog box, as shown in Figure 32.1.
3. Click the RefEdit button in the Array1 entry box.
4. Drag the mouse over the range of cells (B2 through B21) you want included in the analysis. Click the RefEdit button.
5. Click the RefEdit button in the Array2 entry box.
6. Drag the mouse over the range of cells (C2 through C21) you want included in the analysis. Click the RefEdit button.
7. In the Tails entry box, enter the value 2, and in the Type entry box, enter the value 1 (for a paired t-Test).
8. Click OK. The T.TEST function returns its value of 0.145 in Cell C23, as you see in Figure 32.2, indicating that the probability of the associated *t* value occurring by chance alone is .145. Note that you can see the syntax for the function in the formula bar at the top of the worksheet.

Related Functions: F.DIST, F.TEST, T.DIST, Z.TEST

Figure 32.1	The T.TEST Function Arguments Dialog Box

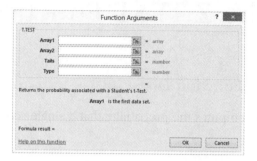

Figure 32.2	The T.TEST Function Returning the Probability of the Student's *t* Value

Check Your Understanding

To check your understanding of the T.TEST function, do the following two problems and check your answers in Appendix A.

QS32a. Compute the probability associated with a t-test for the difference between two methods of training how to speak a foreign language on a test with scores ranging from 0 to 100 for 25 English-speaking, elementary-aged children. Use Data Set 32a.

QS32b. Compute the probability associated with a t-test that Dish 1 is better than Dish 2 for two dishes cooked by 10 chefs, with the outcome variable being a 5-point scale, where 5 = *like very much*, as judged by expert chefs. Use Data Set 32b.

EXCEL QUICKGUIDE 33

The Z.TEST Function

What the Z.TEST Function Does

The Z.TEST function computes the probability that a single score belongs to a population of scores.

The Data Set

The data set used in this example is titled Z.TEST, and the question is, "Does a score of 82 belong to the population set of scores?"

Variable	Description
Memo	Score on a recall memory test ranging from 0 to 100
X	The score to be tested
Sigma	The population standard deviation (computed using the STDEV.P function)

Using the Z.TEST Function

1. Click the cell where you want the Z.TEST function to return its value. (In the data set, the cell is B18.)
2. Select the Formulas tab and click the Insert Function button (*fx*), locate and double-click the Z.TEST function, and you will see the Function Arguments dialog box, as shown in Figure 33.1.
3. Click the RefEdit button in the Array entry box.
4. Drag the mouse over the range of cells (B2 through B16) you want included in the analysis. Click the RefEdit button.
5. Click the RefEdit button in the X entry box and click the *X* value for which you want to compute the *Z* test (Cell C2). Click the RefEdit button.
6. Click the RefEdit button and click the population standard deviation (Cell D2). Click the RefEdit button.
7. Click OK. The Z.TEST function returns its value of 0.94 in Cell B18, as you see in Figure 33.2, indicating that it is highly likely that the *X* value belongs

to the set of sample scores and is not unique. Note that you can see the syntax for the function in the formula bar at the top of the worksheet.

Related Functions: F.DIST, F.TEST, T.DIST, T.TEST

Figure 33.1	The Z.TEST Function Arguments Dialog Box

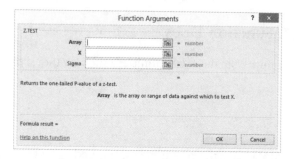

Figure 33.2	The Z.TEST Function Returning the Probability of a Single Value

	A	B	C	D	E	F	G	H
B18		fx	=Z.TEST(B2:B16,C2,D2)					
1	ID	MEMO	X	Sigma				
2	1	67	82	11.44				
3	2	67						
4	3	87						
5	4	89						
6	5	87						
7	6	77						
8	7	73						
9	8	74						
10	9	68						
11	10	72						
12	11	58						
13	12	98						
14	13	98						
15	14	70						
16	15	77						
17								
18	Z.TEST	0.94						

Check Your Understanding

To check your understanding of the Z.TEST function, do the following two problems and check your answers in Appendix A.

QS33a. Compute the probability that a math test score of 83 is characteristic of a set of test scores. Use Data Set 33a.

QS33b. Compute the probability that a free-throw shooting percentage of 63 is unique among conference teams. Use Data Set 33b.

EXCEL QUICKGUIDE 34

The SMALL Function

What the SMALL Function Does

The SMALL function returns smallest kth number (such as the 10th or 15th smallest) in a set of data.

The Data Set

The data set is titled SMALL, and the question being asked is, "What is the 10th smallest number for height in inches, weight in pounds, and friendliness rating for a group of 100 young adults?"

Variable	Value
Height	Height in inches
Weight	Weight in pounds
Status	Rating of friendliness by peers

Using the SMALL Function

1. Click the cell where you want the SMALL function to be placed. (In the data set, the cell is B103.)

2. Select the Formulas tab and click the Insert Function button (*fx*), and locate and double-click the SMALL function. You will see the Function Arguments dialog box, as shown in Figure 34.1.

3. Click the RefEdit button in the Array entry box and enter the range of the cells that contains the criterion. In this example, the range is B2:B101. Click the RefEdit button.

4. In the X entry box, enter the rank of the smallest value, which in this example is 10.

5. Click OK. The SMALL function returns a value of 50 in Cell B103, as you see in Figure 34.2, indicating that the 10th smallest number for the variable height

is 50. Copy the function to Cells C103 and D103, and the 10th smallest values for weight and status are 129 and 1, respectively. Note that you can see the syntax for the function in the formula bar at the top of the worksheet.

Related Functions: COUNT, COUNTA, COUNTBLANK, COUNTIF

| Figure 34.1 | The SMALL Function Arguments Dialog Box |

| Figure 34.2 | The SMALL Function Returning the 10th Smallest Value for the Variable Height |

	A	B	C	D
89	88	55	246	10
90	89	52	247	4
91	90	70	177	10
92	91	63	190	8
93	92	72	173	8
94	93	76	111	1
95	94	64	270	5
96	95	55	212	7
97	96	49	249	9
98	97	53	266	6
99	98	63	270	7
100	99	76	161	3
101	100	55	7	4
102				
103	SMALL	50	129	1

Check Your Understanding

To check your understanding of the SMALL function, do the following two problems and check your answers in Appendix A.

QS34a. Compute the 5th smallest income from a set of 25 university presidents. Use Data Set 34a.

QS34b. Compute the 3rd smallest score for average points scored per game for 10 teams in the IRC Conference. Use Data Set 34b.

EXCEL QUICKGUIDE 35

The LARGE Function

What the LARGE Function Does

The LARGE function returns the largest kth number (such as the 3rd or 20th largest) in a set of data.

The Data Set

The data set is titled LARGE, and the question being asked is, "What is the seventh largest number for memory recall among a group of 50 seniors on a scale from to 100?"

Variable	Value
Score	Score on a memory recall task ranging from 1 to 10

Using the LARGE Function

1. Click the cell where you want the LARGE function to be placed. (In the data set, the cell is B53.)

2. Select the Formulas tab and click the Insert Function button (*fx*), and locate and double-click the LARGE function. You will see the Function Arguments dialog box, as shown in Figure 35.1.

3. Click the RefEdit button in the Array entry box and enter the range of the cells that contains the criterion. In this example, the range is B2:B51. Click the RefEdit button.

4. In the X entry box, enter the rank of the smallest value, which in this example is 7.

5. Click OK. The LARGE function returns a value of 80 in Cell B53, as you see in Figure 35.2, indicating that the seventh smallest score for the recall variable is 80. Note that you can see the syntax for the function in the formula bar at the top of the worksheet.

Related Functions: COUNT, COUNTA, COUNTBLANK, COUNTIF

Figure 35.1	The LARGE Function Arguments Dialog Box

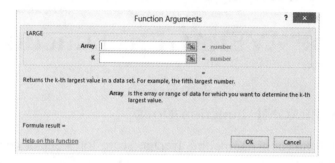

Figure 35.2	The LARGE Function Returning the Average of Males' Scores

B53   × ✓ *fx*   =LARGE(B2:B51,7)

	A	B	C	D	E
31	30	15			
32	31	46			
33	32	49			
34	33	80			
35	34	66			
36	35	69			
37	36	59			
38	37	76			
39	38	74			
40	39	10			
41	40	59			
42	41	19			
43	42	33			
44	43	100			
45	44	60			
46	45	49			
47	46	75			
48	47	14			
49	48	67			
50	49	55			
51	50	69			
52					
53	LARGE	80			

Check Your Understanding

To check your understanding of the LARGE function, do the following two problems and check your answers in Appendix A.

QS35a. What is the ID number of the individual(s) with the 23rd highest score? Use Data Set 35a.

QS35b. Compute the 10th largest value for a set of 25 reaction times. Use Data Set 35b.

EXCEL QUICKGUIDE 36

The AVERAGEIF Function

What the AVERAGEIF Function Does

The AVERAGEIF function returns the average score for a set of cells based on a specific criterion.

The Data Set

The data set is titled AVERAGEIF, and the question being asked is, "What is the average spelling score for males?"

Variable	Value
Gender	Male = 1, female = 2
Test score	Score on a 20-item spelling test

Using the AVERAGEIF Function

1. Click the cell where you want the AVERAGEIF function to be placed. (In the data set, the cell is B28.)

2. Select the Formulas tab and click the Insert Function button (*fx*), and locate and double-click the AVERAGEIF function. You will see the Function Arguments dialog box, as shown in Figure 36.1.

3. Click the RefEdit button in the Range entry box and enter the range of the cells that contains the criterion. In this example, the range is A2:A26. Click the RefEdit button.

4. In the Criteria entry box, enter the selection criterion, which in this case is 1 (for male).

5. Click the RefEdit button in the Average_range entry box and enter the range of the cells for which you want to compute the average (B2:B26). Click the RefEdit button.

6. Click OK. The AVERAGEIF function returns a value of 14.73 in Cell B28, as you see in Figure 36.2, indicating that the average score for males on the 20-item spelling test is 14.73. Note that you can see the syntax for the function in the formula bar at the top of the worksheet.

Related Functions: COUNT, COUNTA, COUNTBLANK, COUNTIF

| Figure 36.1 | The AVERAGEIF Function Arguments Dialog Box |

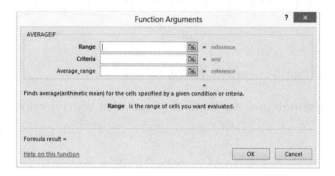

| Figure 36.2 | The AVERAGEIF Function Returning the Average of Males' Scores |

B28   fx   =AVERAGEIF(A2:A26,1,B2:B26)

	A	B	C	D	E	F	G
10	2	14					
11	1	12					
12	2	7					
13	1	16					
14	2	10					
15	1	19					
16	1	18					
17	2	16					
18	2	9					
19	1	19					
20	2	7					
21	1	15					
22	1	13					
23	2	13					
24	2	18					
25	1	9					
26	2	8					
27							
28	AVERAGEIF	14.73					

Check Your Understanding

To check your understanding of the AVERAGEIF function, do the following two problems and check your answers in Appendix A.

QS36a. Compute the average sales value for those members of the A Team (denoted with 1). Use Data Set 36a.

QS36b. Compute the average incidence of infections per 1,000 patients in hospitals in communities with fewer than 200,000 residents. Use Data Set 36b.

EXCEL QUICKGUIDE 37

The COUNT Function

What the COUNT Function Does

The COUNT function returns the number of cells that contain values.

The Data Set

The data set is titled COUNT, and the question being asked is, "How many phone calls resulted in a response?"

Variable	Value
Response	1 or blank

Using the COUNT Function

1. Click the cell where you want the COUNT function to be placed. (In the data set, the cell is B30.)

2. Select the Formulas tab and click the Insert Function button (*fx*), and locate and double-click the COUNT function. You will see the Function Arguments dialog box, as shown in Figure 37.1.

3. Click the RefEdit button in the Value1 entry box and enter the range of the cells that contain the values you want to count. In this example, the range is B2:B28.

4. Click the OK button. The COUNT function returns a value of 18 in Cell B30, as you see in Figure 37.2, indicating that 18 of the 28 participants responded. Note that you can see the syntax for the function in the formula bar at the top of the worksheet.

Related Functions: AVERAGEIF, COUNTA, COUNTBLANK, COUNTIF

| Figure 37.1 | The COUNT Function Arguments Dialog Box |

| Figure 37.2 | The COUNT Function Returning the Number of Respondents |

Check Your Understanding

To check your understanding of the COUNT function, do the following two problems and check your answers in Appendix A.

QS37a. Compute the COUNT value for the number of people who purchased insurance. Use Data Set 37a.

QS37b. Compute the COUNT value for the respondents who gave their age and those who gave their years in service. Use Data Set 37b.

EXCEL QUICKGUIDE 38

The COUNTA Function

What the COUNTA Function Does

The COUNTA function returns the number of cells that contain values, including zeros.

The Data Set

The data set is titled COUNTA, and the question being asked is, "For today's sales, how many customers purchased either beans or mac 'n' cheese?"

Variable	Value
Preferred	Beans, mac 'n' cheese

Using the COUNTA Function

1. Click the cell where you want the COUNTA function to be placed. (In the data set, the cell is B28.)

2. Select the Formulas tab and click the Insert Function button (*fx*), locate and double-click the COUNTA function. You will see the Function Arguments dialog box, as shown in Figure 38.1.

3. Click the RefEdit button in the Value1 entry box and enter the range of the cells that contain the values you want to count. In this example, the range is B2:B26. Click the RefEdit button.

4. Click the OK button. The COUNTA function returns a value of 14 in Cell B28, as you see in Figure 38.2, indicating that 14 of the 25 customers purchased one of the two items. Note that you can see the syntax for the function in the formula bar at the top of the worksheet.

Related Functions: AVERAGEIF, COUNT, COUNTBLANK, COUNTIF

Figure 38.1	The COUNTA Function Arguments Dialog Box

Function Arguments ? ×

COUNTA

Value1 |J2d| 🖼 = 0

Value2 🖼 = number

= 0

Counts the number of cells in a range that are not empty.

Value1: value1,value2,... are 1 to 255 arguments representing the values and cells you want to count. Values can be any type of information.

Formula result = 0

Help on this function | OK | Cancel |

Figure 38.2	The COUNTA Function Returning the Number of Participants and Their Preferences

B28 ⋮ ✕ ✓ *fx* =COUNTA(B2:B26)

	A	B	C	D	E
10	9				
11	10	mac 'n cheese			
12	11				
13	12	mac 'n cheese			
14	13				
15	14				
16	15	mac 'n cheese			
17	16				
18	17	beans			
19	18				
20	19	mac 'n cheese			
21	20				
22	21	beans			
23	22				
24	23	mac 'n cheese			
25	24	mac 'n cheese			
26	25	beans			
27					
28	COUNTA	14			

Check Your Understanding

To check your understanding of the COUNTA function, do the following two problems and check your answers in Appendix A.

QS38a. Compute the COUNTA value for the number of people who decided to enroll in an elective class. Use Data Set 38a.

QS38b. Compute the COUNTA value for the number of communities that adopted curbside or alley recycling. Use Data Set 38b.

EXCEL QUICKGUIDE 39

The COUNTBLANK Function

What the COUNTBLANK Function Does

The COUNTBLANK function returns the number of empty cells in a range of cells.

The Data Set

The data set is titled COUNTBLANK, and the question being asked is, "How many people who were contacted did not agree to participate in the experiment?"

Variable	Value
Agreed	1 (agreed) or empty cell

Using the COUNTBLANK Function

1. Click the cell where you want the COUNTBLANK function to be placed. (In the data set, the cell is B23.)

2. Select the Formulas tab and click the Insert Function button (*fx*), and locate and double-click the COUNTBLANK function. You will see the Function Arguments dialog box, as shown in Figure 39.1.

3. Click the RefEdit button in the Range entry box and enter the range of the cells that contain the values you want included. In this example, the range is B2:B21.

4. Click the OK button. The COUNTBLANK function returns a value of 8 in Cell B23, as you see in Figure 39.2, indicating that 8 respondents did not agree to participate. Note that you can see the syntax for the function in the formula bar at the top of the worksheet.

Related Functions: AVERAGEIF, COUNT, COUNTA, COUNTIF

| Figure 39.1 | The COUNTBLANK Function Arguments Dialog Box |

| Figure 39.2 | The COUNTBLANK Function Returning the Number of Respondents Who Did Not Agree to Participate |

Check Your Understanding

To check your understanding of the COUNTBLANK function, do the following two problems and check your answers in Appendix A.

QS39a. Compute the COUNTBLANK value for the number of students from a group of 35 who did not show up in an elective class. Use Data Set 39a.

QS39b. Compute the COUNTBLANK value for the number of communities that do not have adequate tax bases. Use Data Set 39b.

EXCEL QUICKGUIDE 40

The COUNTIF Function

What the COUNTIF Function Does

The COUNTIF function counts the number of cells in a range of cells that meet a certain criterion.

The Data Set

The data set is titled COUNTIF, and the question being asked is, "How many business transactions were evaluated as successful?"

Variable	Value
Successful	1 = yes, 2 = no

Using the COUNTIF Function

1. Click the cell where you want the COUNTIF function to be placed. (In the data set, the cell is B23.)

2. Select the Formulas tab and click the Insert Function button (*fx*), and locate and double-click the COUNTIF function. You will see the Function Arguments dialog box, as shown in Figure 40.1.

3. Click the RefEdit button in the Range entry box and enter the range of the cells that contain the values you want included. In this example, the range is B2:B21. Click the RefEdit button.

4. Enter the value 1 in the Criteria entry box (for successful).

5. Click the OK button. The COUNTIF function returns a value of 13 in Cell B23, as you see in Figure 40.2, indicating that 13 transactions were successful. Note that you can see the syntax for the function in the formula bar at the top of the worksheet.

Related Functions: AVERAGEIF, COUNT, COUNTA, COUNTBLANK

Figure 40.1	The COUNTIF Function Arguments Dialog Box

Figure 40.2	The COUNTIF Function Returning the Number of Successful Transactions

	A	B	C	D	E
B23	▼	f_x	=COUNTIF(B2:B21,1)		
10	9	2			
11	10	2			
12	11	1			
13	12	1			
14	13	1			
15	14	2			
16	15	2			
17	16	1			
18	17	1			
19	18	1			
20	19	1			
21	20	1			
22					
23	COUNTIF	13			

Check Your Understanding

To check your understanding of the COUNTIF function, do the following two problems and check your answers in Appendix A.

QS40a. Compute the COUNTIF value for the number of students who were admitted to the program and subsequently enrolled (1 = did enroll, 2 = did not enroll). Use Data Set 40a.

QS40b. Compute the COUNTIF value for the number of businesses that are open on the weekends (1 = yes, 2 = no). Use Data Set 3540b.

PART II

USING THE ANALYSIS TOOLPAK

The Excel Analysis ToolPak is a set of automated tools that allows you to conduct a variety of simple and complex statistical analyses. They are similar to Excel functions in that each requires input from the user, but they produce much more elaborate output rather than just one outcome (as do most functions).

For example, the Descriptive Statistics tool in the Analysis ToolPak produces the mean, median, and mode, among other descriptive measures. To compute such values using functions, you would have to use at least three different functions. With the ToolPak, you can do it (and more) by using only one.

Installing the Analysis ToolPak

The Analysis ToolPak is an Excel add-in. An add-in is a program that adds custom commands and features to Microsoft Office. However, if it is not available under the Data tab on the ribbon, it can be installed as follows. If not, be sure to check with your professor as to its availability. If you need to load the Analysis ToolPak into Excel, follow these steps:

1. Select the File tab and then click Options.

2. Click Add-Ins and then, in the Manage box, select "Excel Add-ins."

3. Click Go.

4. In the Add-Ins dialog box, select the Analysis ToolPak checkbox and then click OK.

Using the Analysis ToolPak Tools

The basic method for using any one of the ToolPak tools is as follows:

1. From the Data tab, select the Data Analysis option.

2. Select the tool you want to use.

3. Enter the data and the type of the analysis you want done.

4. Format the data as you see fit. In the examples used in this part of *Excel Statistics: A Quick Guide*, the data may have been reformatted to appear more pleasing to the eye and to be more internally consistent (e.g., numbers are formatted to two decimal places, labels may be centered when appropriate).

The process is very much like using a function, including use of the RefEdit button to enter data into the Function Arguments dialog box, but you may have to make a number of decisions as you prepare the analysis. Among these are the following:

1. Whether you want labels to be used in the Analysis ToolPak output

2. Whether you want the output to appear on the current Excel worksheet, on a new worksheet, or in an entirely new workbook

3. Whether the results should be grouped by columns or rows

4. The range of cells in which you want the output to appear

5. Whether you will enter data in the Data Analysis dialog box rather than using the RefEdit button and dragging over the data

For our purposes here, we will always use labels, have the output appear on the same worksheet, and group the output by columns. The range of cells in which the output should appear will be defined as each Analysis ToolPak tool is discussed. The final or partial output you see will always be reformatted to better fit the page.

Once the Analysis ToolPak output is complete, it can be manipulated as any Excel data can. In addition to being cut and pasted into other applications, such as Word, the output can easily be modified using Excel's Format as Table option on the Home tab. For example, the simple output you saw in Figure 17.2 can easily be reformatted to appear as shown in Figure II.1.

| Figure II.1 | Modifying Excel Analysis ToolPak Output |

ID	Height	Weight
1	60	134
2	63	143
3	71	156
4	58	121
5	61	131
6	59	117
7	64	125
8	67	126
9	63	143
10	52	98
11	61	154
12	58	125
13	54	109
14	61	117
15	64	126
16	63	154
17	49	98
18	59	143
19	69	144
20	71	156
CORREL		0.776

EXCEL QUICKGUIDE 41

Descriptive Statistics

What the Descriptive Statistics Tool Does

The Descriptive Statistics tool computes basic descriptive statistics for a set of data, such as the mean, median, and mode, among others.

The Data Set

The data set used in this example is titled DESCRIPTIVE STATISTICS, and the question is, "What are the descriptive statistics for height for a group of twenty 2-year-olds?"

Variable	Description
Height	Height in inches of 2-year-olds

Using the Descriptive Statistics Tool

1. Select the Data Analysis option from the Data tab.

2. Double-click the Descriptive Statistics option in the Data Analysis dialog box, and you will see the Descriptive Statistics dialog box, as shown in Figure 41.1.

3. Define the Input Range by clicking the RefEdit button and selecting the data you want to use in the analysis (in this example, Cells A1 through A21). Click the RefEdit button again. Be sure to check the Labels in First Row box.

4. Click the Output Range radio button, click the RefEdit button, and define the output range by selecting an area in the worksheet where you want the output to appear (in this example, Cell C2). Click the RefEdit button once again. Even though the range is only one cell, Excel will know to extend it to fit all the output.

5. Click the Summary statistics option and click OK.

The Final Output

The Descriptive Statistics output, including the original data and the summary statistics, is shown in Figure 41.2. Note that the cells were formatted where appropriate using the Format Cells command. Otherwise, Excel produced what you see as the final output.

| Figure 41.1 | The Descriptive Statistics Dialog Box |

| Figure 41.2 | The Descriptive Statistics Output |

Check Your Understanding

To check your understanding of the Descriptive Statistics tool, do the following two problems and check your answers in Figures A.1 and A.2 in Appendix A.

QS41a. Compute the descriptive statistics for a group of cities and their sales tax rates. Use Data Set 41a.

QS41b. Compute the descriptive statistics for number of car sales for 4 weeks in the month of June. Use Data Set 41b.

EXCEL QUICKGUIDE 42

Moving Average

What the Moving Average Tool Does

The Moving Average tool computes the average for sets of numbers at a defined interval.

The Data Set

The data set used in this example is titled MOVING AVERAGE, and the question is, "What is the moving average of number of home sales for subsequent 4-week periods?"

Variable	Description
Sales	Number of home sales in a 1-week period

Using the Moving Average Tool

1. Select the Data Analysis option from the Data tab.

2. Double-click the Moving Average option in the Data Analysis dialog box, and you will see the Moving Average dialog box shown in Figure 42.1.

3. Define the Input Range by clicking the RefEdit button and selecting the data you want to use in the analysis (in this example, Cells B1 through B13). Click the RefEdit button once again. Be sure to check the Labels in First Row box.

4. Define the Interval, or the number of values you want to be included in the calculation of each average. In this example, enter 4 directly in the dialog box.

5. Click the Output Range radio button, click the RefEdit button, and select an area in the worksheet where you want the output to appear (in this example, Cell D1). Click the RefEdit button once again. Even though the range is only one cell, Excel will know to extend it to fit all the output.

6. Check the Chart Output checkbox and click OK.

The Final Output

The Moving Average output, including the original data and the averages, is shown in Figure 42.2. As you can see, the first three averages are marked "#N/A" because Excel must detect four averages before it can compute the first one. Otherwise, Excel produces what you see as the final output.

Figure 42.1	The Moving Average Dialog Box

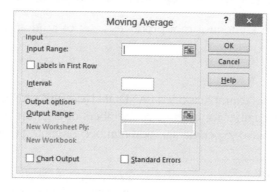

Figure 42.2	The Moving Average Output

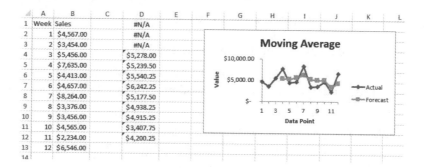

Check Your Understanding

To check your understanding of the Moving Average tool, do the following two problems and check your answers in Figures A.3 and A.4 in Appendix A.

QS42a. Compute the moving average of the use of parking spaces in a 100-space lot for adjacent 4-month periods. Use Data Set 42a and an interval of 4.

QS42b. Compute the moving average of hours of training for each 5-week period over 12 weeks. Use Data Set 42b and an interval of 2.

EXCEL QUICKGUIDE 43

Random Number Generator

What the Random Number Generator Tool Does

The Random Number Generator tool produces a set of random numbers.

The Data Set

The data set used in this example is titled RANDOM NUMBER GENERATOR, and the tool generates a random number for each of 20 members of a group. The numbers will be used to assign members to experimental (odd number) or control (even number) groups.

Variable	Description
ID	Participant's identifying number
Random Number	Random number assigned to each ID

Using the Random Number Generator Tool

1. Select the Data Analysis option from the Data tab.
2. Double-click the Random Number Generation option in the Data Analysis dialog box, and you will see the Random Number Generation dialog box shown in Figure 43.1.
3. Define the Number of Variables (in this example, 1).
4. Define the Number of Random Numbers (in this example, 20).
5. Select Normal from the Distribution drop-down menu. The Random Number Generation dialog box changes, offering you entry boxes for Mean and Standard deviation.
6. Enter 1 for Mean.
7. Enter 1 for Standard deviation.
8. Click on the RefEdit button for the Output Range and select the range where you want the random numbers to be placed (in this example, Cells B2 through B21). Click the RefEdit button.
9. Click OK.

The Final Output

The 20 random numbers appear as shown in Figure 43.2. Members with numbers ending in odd digits are to be placed in the experimental group, and members with numbers ending in even digits will be placed in the control group.

| Figure 43.1 | The Random Number Generation Dialog Box |

| Figure 43.2 | The Random Number Generation Output |

	A	B
1	ID	RANDOM NUMBERS
2	1	0.853557711
3	2	0.991011919
4	3	-1.360502549
5	4	2.206230991
6	5	0.066449163
7	6	1.127986368
8	7	0.100675723
9	8	-0.821408659
10	9	1.363694426
11	10	1.311856638
12	11	2.554267328
13	12	1.531532578
14	13	0.459989795
15	14	0.48775212
16	15	-0.075311502
17	16	2.084081305
18	17	-0.912685548
19	18	3.738888725

Check Your Understanding

To check your understanding of the Random Number Generator tool, do the following two problems and check your answers in Figures A.5 and A.6 in Appendix A.

QS43a. Compute a set of 25 random numbers. Use Data Set 43a.

QS43b. Compute a set of 10 random numbers to assign each of 10 participants to one of two groups in an experiment. Use Data Set 43b.

EXCEL QUICKGUIDE 44

Rank and Percentile

What the Rank and Percentile Tool Does

The Rank and Percentile tool produces the point, rank, and percentiles for a set of scores.

The Data Set

The data set used in this example is titled RANK AND PERCENTILE, and the question is, "What are the rank and percentile scores for a set of 10 grade point averages (GPAs)?"

Variable	Description
GPA	GPA ranging from 0.0 to 4.0

Using the Rank and Percentile Tool

1. Select the Data Analysis option from the Data tab.
2. Double-click the Rank and Percentile option in the Data Analysis dialog box, and you will see the Rank and Percentile dialog box shown in Figure 44.1.
3. Be sure that the Columns button and the Labels in First Row checkbox are selected.
4. Click the RefEdit button in the Input Range entry box and select the data you want to use in the analysis (in this example, Cells A1 through A11). Click the RefEdit button again.
5. Click the RefEdit button in the Output Range entry box and select the location where you want the output to appear (in this example, Cell B1). Click the RefEdit button again.
6. Click OK.

The Final Output

The point (the GPA's location in the original set of data), the GPA, the rank, and the percent (percentile) for each GPA in the data set are shown in Figure 44.2.

Figure 44.1   The Rank and Percentile Dialog Box

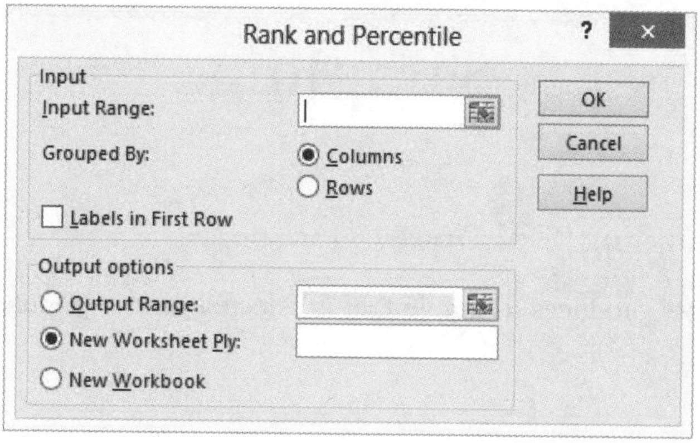

	Rank and Percentile	?	✕
Input			
Input Range:	[＿＿＿＿＿＿] 📇		OK
Grouped By:	● Columns		Cancel
	○ Rows		Help
☐ Labels in First Row			
Output options			
○ Output Range:	[＿＿＿＿＿＿] 📇		
● New Worksheet Ply:	[＿＿＿＿＿＿]		
○ New Workbook			

Figure 44.2   The Rank and Percentile Output

	A	B	C	D	E
1	GPA	*Point*	*GPA*	*Rank*	*Percent*
2	3.8	6	3.9	1	100.00%
3	2.5	1	3.8	2	88.80%
4	3.1	9	3.5	3	77.70%
5	1.6	3	3.1	4	66.60%
6	2.8	5	2.8	5	55.50%
7	3.9	7	2.6	6	44.40%
8	2.6	2	2.5	7	33.30%
9	1.2	10	2.2	8	22.20%
10	3.5	4	1.6	9	11.10%
11	2.2	8	1.2	10	0.00%

Check Your Understanding

To check your understanding of the Rank and Percentile tool, do the following two problems and check your answers in Figures A.7 and A.8 in Appendix A.

    QS44a. Compute the rank and percentile for a group of 20 salaries. Use Data Set 44a.

    QS44b. Compute the rank and percentile for 15 students and the hours studied per week. Use Data Set 44b.

EXCEL QUICKGUIDE 45

Sampling

What the Sampling Tool Does

The Sampling tool produces a sample that is selected from a population.

The Data Set

The data set used in this example is titled SAMPLING, and the question is, "What are the identification numbers of 10 participants selected at random from a population of 200?"

Variable	Description
ID	Identification number

Using the Sampling Tool

1. Select the Data Analysis option from the Data tab.
2. Double-click the Sampling option in the Data Analysis dialog box, and you will see the Sampling dialog box shown in Figure 45.1.
3. Click the RefEdit button in the Input Range entry box and select the data you want to use in the analysis (in this example, Cells A2 through J21). Click the RefEdit button again.
4. Click the Random button and enter the number you want randomly selected. In this example, the number is 10.
5. Click the RefEdit button in the Output Range entry box and select the location where you want the output to appear (in this example, Cell L2). Click the RefEdit button again.
6. Click OK.

The Final Output

The 10 ID numbers randomly selected are shown in Figure 45.2.

Figure 45.1	The Sampling Dialog Box

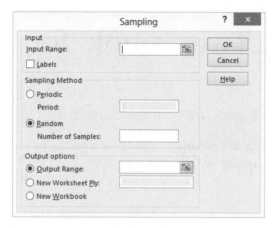

Figure 45.2	The Sampling Output

	A	B	C	D	E	F	G	H	I	J	K	L
1	ID											Sample
2	43	61	32	72	43	25	32	94	97	42		60
3	42	60	23	68	71	69	29	95	65	31		50
4	81	43	13	19	100	41	81	10	6	53		6
5	60	9	7	43	88	65	13	94	3	53		74
6	88	81	40	62	43	29	97	76	65	27		27
7	14	11	80	52	88	88	45	74	59	84		22
8	25	10	97	96	6	54	42	45	88	97		44
9	80	21	40	9	37	88	97	97	85	17		13
10	13	8	34	50	46	23	93	29	50	63		37
11	68	11	18	92	65	53	88	44	95	82		9
12	62	10	40	6	74	17	9	31	38	93		
13	77	16	73	20	13	97	76	79	34	32		
14	37	88	27	21	39	61	65	42	93	11		
15	86	14	64	38	34	68	16	30	47	41		
16	67	93	13	52	4	68	12	21	41	15		
17	15	94	61	77	22	76	43	79	14	14		
18	70	17	95	5	18	28	37	88	94	64		
19	74	85	96	94	62	32	11	62	65	22		
20	81	93	77	17	10	97	33	23	68	34		
21	12	53	88	8	76	82	45	9	62	16		

Check Your Understanding

To check your understanding of the Sampling tool, do the following two problems and check your answers in Figures A.9 and A.10 in Appendix A.

QS45a. Select a random sample of 15 participants from a population of 90 with values between 50 and 150. Use Data Set 45a.

QS45b. Select a random sample of 20 from a population of 100 with values between 1 and 1,000. Use Data Set 45b.

EXCEL QUICKGUIDE 46

z-Test: Two-Sample for Means

What the z-Test: Two-Sample for Means Tool Does

The z-Test: Two-Sample for Means computes a z value between means when the population variances are known.

The Data Set

The data set used in this example is titled ZTEST, and the question is, "Do the population means for urban and rural residents differ on a test of energy use?"

Variable	Description
Energy Use	Total annual energy costs in dollars

Using the z-Test: Two-Sample for Means Tool

1. Select the Data Analysis option from the Data tab.
2. Double-click the z-Test: Two-Sample for Means option in the Data Analysis dialog box, and you will see the z-Test: Two-Sample for Means dialog box shown in Figure 46.1.
3. Be sure that the Labels box in the Input area is checked.
4. Click the RefEdit button in the Variable 1 Range entry box and select the data you want to use in the analysis. In this example, it is Cells B1 through B21. Click the RefEdit button again.
5. Repeat Step 4 for the Variable 2 Range entry box and select the data you want to use in the analysis. In this example, it is Cells C1 through C21. Click the RefEdit button again.
6. Enter the known population variance for both arrays of data in Variable 1 Variance (known) and Variable 2 Variance (known), respectively. In this example, VAR.P was used to compute these values, which are available in Cells B23 and C23.
7. Click the RefEdit button and enter the output range. In this example, Cell D1 was selected. Click the RefEdit button again.
8. Click OK.

The Final Output

The result, shown in Cell E8 of Figure 46.2, is a z value of 5.12, which is significant beyond the .05 level. This indicates that urban and rural residents differ in their energy use.

Figure 46.1	The z-Test: Two-Sample for Means Dialog Box

Figure 46.2	The z-Test: Two-Sample for Means Output

Check Your Understanding

To check your understanding of the z-Test: Two-Sample for Means tool, do the following two problems and check your answers in Figures A.11 and A.12 in Appendix A.

QS46a. Compute the z value and evaluate it for significance for the scores on an attitude scale ranging from 1 to 5 (with 5 being most satisfied) between two groups of 20 homeowners. Use Data Set 46a.

QS46b. Compute the z value and evaluate it for significance for the heaviest single lift between two groups of 15 participants in a program to increase strength. Use Data Set 46b.

EXCEL QUICKGUIDE 47

t-Test: Paired
Two-Sample for Means

What the t-Test: Paired Two-Sample for Means Tool Does

The t-Test: Paired Two-Sample for Means computes a *t* value between means for two dependent measures on the same individuals or set of cases.

The Data Set

The data set used in this example is titled TTEST-PAIRED, and the question is "Does an intervention program reduce the number of cigarettes smoked each day?"

Variable	Description
Before	Number of cigarettes smoked before the intervention
After	Number of cigarettes smoked after the intervention

Using the t-Test: Paired Two-Sample for Means Tool

1. Select the Data Analysis option from the Data tab.
2. Double-click the t-Test: Paired Two-Sample for Means option in the Data Analysis dialog box, and you will see the t-Test: Paired Two-Sample for Means dialog box shown in Figure 47.1.
3. Click the RefEdit button in the Variable 1 Range entry box and select the data you want to use in the analysis. In this example, it is Cells A1 through A21. Click the RefEdit button again.
4. Repeat Step 3 for the Variable 2 Range entry box and select the data you want to use in the analysis. In this example, it is Cells B1 through B21. Click the RefEdit button again.
5. Be sure that the Labels box in the Input area is checked.
6. Be sure that an Alpha value of 0.05 is selected.
7. Click the RefEdit button and enter the Output Range. In this example, Cell C1 is selected. Click the RefEdit button again.
8. Click OK.

The Final Output

The result, shown in Figure 47.2, is a *t* value of 6.27, which is significant beyond the .05 level (the alpha value in Figure 47.1). This indicates that the intervention was effective and there was a difference in rate of daily cigarette smoking.

Figure 47.1	The t-Test: Paired Two-Sample for Means Dialog Box

Figure 47.2	The t-Test: Paired Two-Sample for Means Output

Check Your Understanding

To check your understanding of the t-Test: Paired Two-Sample for Means tool, do the following two problems and check your answers in Figures A.13 and A.14 in Appendix A.

QS47a. Compute the *t* value and evaluate it for significance for law school admission scores for the same group of 25 participants before and after a crash study course. Use Data Set 47a.

QS47b. Compute the *t* value and evaluate it for significance for body mass index scores for 20 participants in a wellness program before and after the program. Use Data Set 47b.

EXCEL QUICKGUIDE 48

t-Test: Two-Sample Assuming Unequal Variances

What the t-Test: Two-Sample Assuming Unequal Variances Tool Does

The t-Test: Two-Sample Assuming Unequal Variances tool computes a *t* value between means for two independent measures when the variances for each group are unequal.

The Data Set

The data set used in this example is titled TTEST-UNEQUAL, and the question is, "Is there a difference in contribution levels to nonprofits between married and never-married females?"

Variable	Description
Married females	Amount of money donated to not-for-profit organizations in dollars per year by married females
Never married females	Amount of money donated to not-for-profit organizations in dollars per year by never-married females

Using the t-Test: Two-Sample Assuming Unequal Variances Tool

1. Select the Data Analysis option from the Data tab.

2. Double-click the t-Test: Two-Sample Assuming Unequal Variances option in the Data Analysis dialog box, and you will see the t-Test: Two-Sample Assuming Unequal Variances dialog box shown in Figure 48.1.

3. Click the RefEdit button in the Variable 1 Range entry box and select the data you want to use in the analysis. In this example, it is Cells A1 through A21. Click the RefEdit button again.

4. Repeat Step 3 for the Variable 2 Range entry box and select the data you want to use in the analysis. In this example, it is Cells B1 through B23. Click the RefEdit button again.

5. Be sure that the Labels box in the Input area is checked.

6. Click the RefEdit button and enter the Output Range. In this example, Cell C1 was selected. Click the RefEdit button again.

7. Click OK.

The Final Output

The result, shown in Figure 48.2, is a *t* value of –0.28, which is not significant beyond the .05 level. This indicates that there is no difference in the amount of dollars contributed to nonprofit organizations by married and never-married females.

Figure 48.1	The t-Test: Two-Sample Assuming Unequal Variances Dialog Box

Figure 48.2	The t-Test: Two-Sample Assuming Unequal Variances Output

	A	B	C	D	E
1	Married Females	Never Married Females	t-Test: Two-Sample Assuming Unequal Variances		
2	$ 1,342	$ 2,546			
3	$ 2,413	$ 1,867		Married Females	Never Married Females
4	$ 657	$ 3,354	Mean	1862.95	1972.82
5	$ 456	$ 2,176	Variance	2731592.37	441235.11
6	$ 4,132	$ 2,657	Observations	20	22
7	$ 2,154	$ 2,345	Hypothesized Mean Difference	0	
8	$ 768	$ 1,878	df	25	
9	$ 454	$ 1,677	t Stat	-0.28	
10	$ 1,654	$ 1,164	P(T<=t) one-tail	0.39	
11	$ 3,321	$ 1,987	t Critical one-tail	1.71	
12	$ 1,213	$ 1,988	P(T<=t) two-tail	0.78	
13	$ 198	$ 2,165	t Critical two-tail	2.06	
14	$ 278	$ 2,645			
15	$ 6,132	$ 1,134			
16	$ 4,325	$ 2,123			
17	$ 1,545	$ 2,241			
18	$ 33	$ 1,989			
19	$ 2,143	$ 2,242			
20	$ 654	$ 1,546			
21	$ 3,387	$ 345			
22		$ 2,454			
23		$ 879			

Check Your Understanding

To check your understanding of the t-Test: Two-Sample Assuming Unequal Variables, do the following two problems and check your answers in Figures A.15 and A.16 in Appendix A.

QS48a. Compute the *t* value and evaluate it for the significance in differences in infant mortality rates (per 1,000 live births) between two different groups of countries. Use Data Set 48a.

QS48b. Compute the *t* value and evaluate it for the significance in differences in amount of student debt after 10 years between private and public debt. Use Data Set 48b.

EXCEL QUICKGUIDE 49

t-Test: Two-Sample Assuming Equal Variances

What the t-Test: Two-Sample Assuming Equal Variances Tool Does

The t-Test: Two-Sample Assuming Equal Variances tool computes a *t* value between means for two independent measures when the variances for each group are equal.

The Data Set

The data set used in this example is titled TTEST-EQUAL, and the question is, "Is there a difference in weekly sales of units between Region 1 and Region 2?"

Variable	Description
Sales R1	Weekly sales in units for Region 1
Sales R2	Weekly sales in units for Region 2

Using the t-Test: Two-Sample Assuming Equal Variances Tool

1. Select the Data Analysis option from the Data tab.
2. Double-click the t-Test: Two-Sample Assuming Equal Variances option in the Data Analysis dialog box, and you will see the t-Test: Two-Sample Assuming Equal Variances dialog box shown in Figure 49.1.
3. Click the RefEdit button in the Variable 1 Range entry box and select the data you want to use in the analysis. In this example, it is Cells B1 through B17. Click the RefEdit button.
4. Repeat Step 3 for the Variable 2 Range entry box and select the data you want to use in the analysis. In this example, it is Cells C1 through C17. Click the RefEdit button.
5. Be sure that the Labels box in the Input area is checked.
· 6. Click the RefEdit button and enter the Output Range. In this example, Cell D1 was selected. Click the RefEdit button again.
7. Click OK.

The Final Output

The result, shown in Figure 49.2, is a t value of -2.76, which is significant beyond the .05 level (as specified in the dialog box you see in Figure 49.1) for a two-tailed test. This indicates that there is a difference in sales between the two regions.

Figure 49.1	The t-Test: Two-Sample Assuming Equal Variances Dialog Box

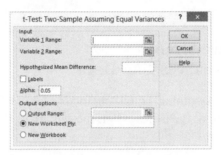

Figure 49.2	The t-Test: Two-Sample Assuming Equal Variances Output

	A	B	C	D	E	F
1	Week	Sales R1	Sales R2	t-Test: Two-Sample Assuming Equal Variances		
2	1	$ 465	$ 657			
3	2	$ 465	$ 789		Sales R1	Sales R2
4	3	$ 423	$ 456	Mean	$ 408.56	$ 531.69
5	4	$ 398	$ 655	Variance	$ 3,013.06	$ 28,745.56
6	5	$ 387	$ 354	Observations	16	16
7	6	$ 416	$ 775	Pooled Variance	$ 15,879.31	
8	7	$ 401	$ 726	Hypothesized Mean Difference	0	
9	8	$ 326	$ 389	df	30	
10	9	$ 345	$ 456	t Stat	-2.76	
11	10	$ 476	$ 331	P(T<=t) one-tail	0.00	
12	11	$ 312	$ 412	t Critical one-tail	1.70	
13	12	$ 334	$ 588	P(T<=t) two-tail	0.01	
14	13	$ 431	$ 312	t Critical two-tail	2.04	
15	14	$ 478	$ 331			
16	15	$ 453	$ 589			
17	16	$ 427	$ 687			

Check Your Understanding

To check your understanding of the t-Test: Two Samples Assuming Equal Variances, do the following two problems and check your answers in Figures A.17 and A.18 in Appendix A.

QS49a. Compute the t value and evaluate it for significance for the difference between the number of cigarettes smoked each day between two groups, one of which is in a smoking cessation program and the other is a control group. Use Data Set 49a.

QS49b. Compute the t value and evaluate it for significance for the difference between 25 salaries of graduates of online versus bricks-and-mortar master's degree programs. Use Data Set 49b.

EXCEL QUICKGUIDE 50

Anova: Single Factor

What the Anova: Single Factor Tool Does

The Anova: Single Factor tool tests for differences between the means of two or more groups.

The Data Set

The data set used in this example is titled Anova-Single Factor, and the question is, "Is there a difference in language proficiency as a function of number of hours of weekly practice?"

Variable	Description
LP	Language proficiency
Practice	Number of hours of practice, either 5 or 10 per week

Using the Anova: Single Factor Tool

1. Select the Data Analysis option from the Data tab.
2. Double-click the Anova: Single Factor option in the Data Analysis dialog box, and you will see the Anova: Single Factor dialog box shown in Figure 50.1.
3. Click the RefEdit button in the Input Range entry box and select the data you want to use in the analysis. In this example, it is Cells A1 through C21. Click the RefEdit button again.
4. Be sure to check the Labels in First Row box.
5. Click the RefEdit button and enter the Output Range. In this example, Cell D1 was selected. Click the RefEdit button again.
6. Click OK.

The Final Output

The result, shown in Figure 50.2, shows language proficiency increasing with more practice and the difference between the means of the three groups being significant at the .02 level, given an *F* value of 4.45.

Figure 50.1 The Anova: Single Factor Dialog Box

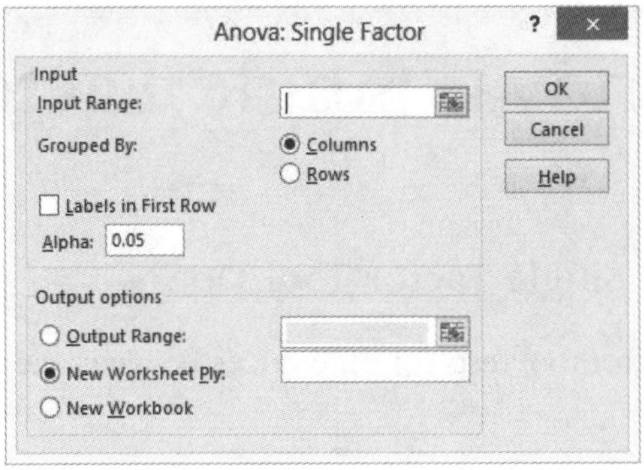

Figure 50.2 The Anova: Single Factor Output

	A	B	C	D	E	F	G	H	I	J
1	No Practice	5 Hours	10 Hours	Anova: Single Factor						
2	7	7	15							
3	11	8	18	SUMMARY						
4	13	9	15	Groups	Count	Sum	verag	ariance		
5	12	10	11	No Practice	20	205	10.3	18.51		
6	6	12	16	5 Hours	20	233	11.7	13.40		
7	4	15	15	10 Hours	20	278	13.9	13.78		
8	7	11	9							
9	8	12	10							
10	16	9	12	ANOVA						
11	11	8	8	Source of Variation	SS	df	MS	F	-valu	F crit
12	9	10	19	Between Groups	135.63	2	67.82	4.45	0.02	3.16
13	6	7	16	Within Groups	868.10	57	15.23			
14	15	15	6							
15	13	14	19	Total	1003.73	59				
16	11	17	17							
17	11	16	13							
18	7	20	18							
19	16	11	14							
20	19	14	15							
21	3	8	12							

Check Your Understanding

To check your understanding of the Anova: Single Factor tool, do the following two problems and check your answers in Figures A.19 and A.20 in Appendix A.

QS50a. Compute the F value and evaluate it for significance for end-of-year math scores (out of 100 possible points) for three groups of home-schooled children in different enrichment programs. Use Data Set 50a.

QS50b. Compute the F value and evaluate it for significance for four different levels of participation in a program that is designed to increase self-esteem on a measure of extroversion and introversion that ranges from 1 to 10, with 10 indicating high self-esteem. Use Data Set 50b.

EXCEL QUICKGUIDE 51

Anova: Two-Factor With Replication

What the Anova: Two-Factor With Replication Tool Does

The Anova: Two-Factor With Replication tool tests for differences between the means of two or more dependent groups or measures.

The Data Set

The data set used in this example is titled ANOVA WITH REPLICATION, and the question is, "Is there a difference in satisfaction level over four training sessions for 20 unemployed men and women undergoing quarterly training?"

Variable	Description
Gender	Male or female
TQ	Training score for each quarter
SAT	Level of satisfaction from 1 to 100 for each of four quarters

Using the Anova: Two-Factor With Replication Tool

1. Select the Data Analysis option from the Data tab.

2. Double-click the Anova: Two-Factor With Replication option in the Data Analysis dialog box, and you will see the Anova: Two-Factor With Replication dialog box shown in Figure 51.1.

3. Click the RefEdit button in the Input Range entry box and select the data you want to use in the analysis. In this example, it is Cells C2 through F22. Click the RefEdit button.

4. Enter the number of rows in *each* sample in the Rows per sample box. In this case, it is 10.

5. Make sure the Alpha level is set at 0.05.

6. Click the RefEdit button and enter the Output Range. In this example, Cell G1 was selected. Click the RefEdit button again.

7. Click OK.

The Final Output

The results, shown in Figure 51.2, consist of several summary statistics for males and females and three F ratios testing the main effects of training, gender, and the interaction. With F values of 0.73 and 0.52, respectively, for session and the interaction of gender and session, there was no significant outcome. For the main effect of gender ($F = 6.29$), there was a significant outcome showing that regardless of gender, training changed over the four-quarter period. An examination of total means shows that females outperformed males.

Figure 51.1	The Anova: Two-Factor With Replication Dialog Box

Figure 51.2	The Anova: Two-Factor With Replication Output

	A	B	C	D	E	F	G	H	I	J	K	L	M
1				Training Sessions			Anova: Two-Factor With Replication						
2			Session 1	Session2	Session 3	Session 4							
3		Male	1382	1046	1352	1414	SUMMARY		Session 1	Session2	Session 3	Session 4	Total
4			1226	1015	1499	1168	*Male*						
5			1087	1020	1017	1590	Count	10	10	10	10	40	
6			929	1172	1160	1039	Sum	12307	10940	12035	12356	47638	
7			1394	1373	859	1370	Average	1230.70	1094	1203.50	1235.60	1190.95	
8	Gender		1096	1273	1246	1029	Variance	32508.01	32428.44	33175.39	48820.71	37274.31	
9			1499	1049	1325	910							
10			1233	878	1268	1343	*Female*						
11			1374	1292	1219	1420	Count	10	10	10	10	40	
12			1087	822	1090	1073	Sum	13538	13052	12725	13033	52348	
13		Female	1285	1479	1388	1013	Average	1353.80	1305.20	1272.50	1303.30	1308.70	
14			1505	1581	1493	1415	Variance	52020.18	69194.84	40386.72	44015.57	48318.32	
15			1452	1578	1540	1284							
16			1310	1322	1138	1308	*Total*						
17			943	1104	1286	930	Count	20	20	20	20		
18			1525	871	841	1592	Sum	25845	23992	24760	25389		
19			1478	1550	1208	1304	Average	1292.25	1199.60	1238.00	1269.45		
20			1479	1386	1350	1249	Variance	44027.46	59875.62	36098.11	45181.21		
21			973	1255	1159	1373							
22			1588	926	1322	1565							
23							ANOVA						
24							*Source of Variation*	SS	df	MS	F	P-value	F crit
25							Sample	277301	1	277301.25	6.29	0.01	3.97
26							Columns	96948.1	3	32316.02	0.73	0.54	2.73
27							Interaction	68215.4	3	22738.48	0.52	0.67	2.73
28							Within	3172949	72	44068.73			
29													
30							Total	3615414	79				

Check Your Understanding

To check your understanding of the Anova: Two-Factor With Replication tool, do the following two problems and check your answers in Figures A.21 and A.22 in Appendix A.

QS51a. Compute the *F* value and evaluate it for significance between different genders and three levels of program involvement (1-, 5-, and 10-hour weekly supplement) for history achievement on a test score ranging from 1 to 100. Use Data Set 51a.

QS51b. Compute the *F* value and evaluate it for significance between two levels of participation in remedial work (high and low) and two levels of teaching programs on out-of-social school behaviors, as measured by the Out of School (OOS) assessment tool. Scores on the OOS range from 1 to 10, with 10 being most social. Use Data Set 51b.

EXCEL QUICKGUIDE 52

Anova: Two-Factor Without Replication

What the Anova: Two-Factor Without Replication Tool Does

The Anova: Two-Factor Without Replication tool tests for differences between the means of two or more independent groups or measures.

The Data Set

The data set used in this example is titled ANOVA WITHOUT REPLICATION, and the question is, "Does happiness, as measured by the Happiness Scale (HS), differ as a function of where people live (residence) and their political affiliation?"

Variable	Description
Residence	Rural or urban
Political Affiliation	Party 1 or Party 2
HS	Happiness Scale

Using the Anova: Two-Factor Without Replication Tool

1. Select the Data Analysis option from the Data tab.

2. Double-click the Anova: Two-Factor Without Replication option in the Data Analysis dialog box, and you will see the Anova: Two-Factor Without Replication dialog box shown in Figure 52.1.

3. Click the RefEdit button in the Input Range entry box and select the data you want to use in the analysis. In this example, it is Cells B2 through D22. Click the RefEdit button again.

4. Be sure that the Labels box in the Input area is checked.

5. Be sure that the Alpha level is at 0.05.

6. Click the RefEdit button and enter the Output Range. In this example, Cell E1 was selected. Click the RefEdit button again.

7. Click OK.

The Final Output

The results, shown in Figure 52.2, are that the overall *F* value for political affiliation (0.82) is not significant, and the value for residence (4.41) is significant at the .05 level. There is no test of the interaction. The final conclusion is that rural residents (average happiness score of 7.3) are happier than urban residents (average happiness score of 5.9).

Figure 52.1	The Anova: Two-Factor Without Replication Dialog Box

Figure 52.2	The Anova: Two-Factor Without Replication Output

Urban	20	118	5.9	3.88		
Rural	20	146	7.3	4.22		
ANOVA						
Source of Variation	SS	df	MS	F	P-value	F crit
Rows	69.60	19	3.66	0.82	0.66	2.17
Columns	19.60	1	19.60	4.41	0.05	4.38
Error	84.40	19	4.44			
Total	173.60	39				

Check Your Understanding

To check your understanding of the ANOVA: Two Factor Without Replication tool, do the following two problems and check your answers in Figures A.23 and A.24 in Appendix A.

QS52a. Compute the *F* value and evaluate it for significance among three different speaking programs with three different levels of experience (1, 2, and 3), with the outcome variable being number of speeches per year. Use Data Set 52a.

QS52b. Compute the *F* value and evaluate it for significance between different neighborhoods in two communities and two levels of advertising on recycling rates measured from 0 to 100, with 100 representing "recycles as much as possible." Use Data Set 52b.

EXCEL QUICKGUIDE 53

The Correlation Tool

What the Correlation Tool Does

The Correlation tool computes the value of the Pearson product–moment correlation between two variables.

The Data Set

The data set used in this example is titled CORRELATION, and the question is, "What is the correlation between number of years teaching and teaching skills?"

Variable	Description
Years teaching	Number of years teaching
Teaching skills	Teaching skills rated from 1 to 10

Using the Correlation Tool

1. Select the Data Analysis option from the Data tab.
2. Double-click the Correlation option in the Data Analysis dialog box, and you will see the Correlation dialog box shown in Figure 53.1.
3. Click the RefEdit button in the Input Range entry box and select the data you want to use in the analysis. In this example, it is Cells C1 through D21. Click the RefEdit button again.
4. Be sure to check the Labels in First Row box.
5. Click the RefEdit button and enter the Output Range. In this example, Cell D1 is selected. Click the RefEdit button again.
6. Click OK.

The Final Output

The result, shown in Figure 53.2, is a correlation between years teaching and teaching skills of .67.

Figure 53.1 The Correlation Dialog Box

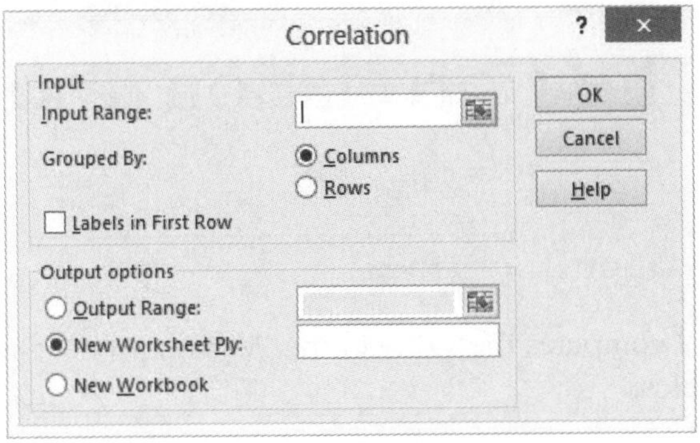

Figure 53.2 The Correlation Output

▲	A	B	C	D	E	F
1	ID	Years Teaching	Teaching Skills		*Years Teaching*	*Teaching Skills*
2	1	14	8	Years Teaching	1	
3	2	21	10	Teaching Skills	0.67	1
4	3	5	6			
5	4	26	9			
6	5	13	8			
7	6	9	6			
8	7	11	9			
9	8	5	5			
10	9	17	9			
11	10	25	9			
12	11	31	9			
13	12	19	7			
14	13	12	9			
15	14	5	8			
16	15	1	3			
17	16	11	7			
18	17	16	8			
19	18	13	9			
20	19	15	9			
21	20	7	8			

Check Your Understanding

To check your understanding of the Correlation tool, do the following two problems and check your answers in Figures A.25 and A.26 in Appendix A.

QS53a. Compute the correlation between consumption of ice cream (times eaten) and crime rate (frequency) in 15 midwestern cities. Use Data Set 53a.

QS53b. Compute the correlation between speed of completing a task and the accuracy with which that task is completed. Use Data Set 53b.

EXCEL QUICKGUIDE 54

The Regression Tool

What the Regression Tool Does

The Regression tool uses a linear regression model to predict a *Y* outcome from an *X* variable.

The Data Set

The data set used in this example is titled REGRESSION, and the question is, "How well does the average number of hours spent studying predict GPA?"

Variable	Description
Hours	Hours of studying each week
GPA	Grade point average

Using the Regression Tool

1. Select the Data Analysis option from the Data tab.

2. Double-click the Regression option in the Data Analysis dialog box, and you will see the Regression dialog box shown in Figure 54.1.

3. Click the RefEdit button in the Input Y Range entry box and select the data you want to use in the analysis. In this example, it is Cells B1 through B21. Click the RefEdit button again.

4. Repeat Step 3 for the Input X Range entry box. In this example, select Cells A1 through A21. Click the RefEdit button again.

5. Be sure to check the Labels box.

6. Check the Confidence Level box and make sure the confidence level is set to 95%.

7. Click the Output Range button, click the RefEdit button, and enter the output range. In this example, Cell C1 is selected. Click the RefEdit button again.

8. Click OK.

The Final Output

The results in Figure 54.2 show the formula for the regression line to be $Y' = 0.05x + 1.64$.

Figure 54.1 The Regression Dialog Box

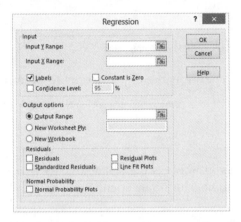

Figure 54.2 The Regression Output

	A	B	C	D	E	F	G	H	I	J	K
1	Hours (X)	GPA (Y)	SUMMARY OUTPUT								
2	15	3.4									
3	11	2.1	*Regression Statistics*								
4	21	2.8	Multiple R	0.51							
5	25	3.7	R Square	0.26							
6	24	2.1	Adjusted R Square	0.22							
7	17	1.8	Standard Error	0.64							
8	9	1.3	Observations	20							
9	25	3.2									
10	21	3.7	ANOVA								
11	22	2.8		*df*	*SS*	*MS*	*F*	*Significance F*			
12	18	2.1	Regression	1	2.59	2.59	6.26	0.02			
13	13	2.9	Residual	18	7.45	0.41					
14	27	3.1	Total	19	10.038						
15	16	1.9									
16	31	3.3		*Coefficients*	*Standard Error*	*t Stat*	*P-value*	*Lower 95%*	*Upper 95%*	*Lower 95.0%*	*Upper 95.0%*
17	36	3.8	Intercept	1.64	0.45	3.65	0.00	0.70	2.59	0.70	2.59
18	22	2.8	Hours (X)	0.05	0.02	2.50	0.02	0.01	0.10	0.01	0.10
19	23	1.8									
20	21	2.5									
21	9	3.1									

Check Your Understanding

To check your understanding of the Regression tool, do the following two problems and check your answers in Figures A.27 and A.28 in Appendix A.

QS54a. Compute the regression line for predicting wins from number of injuries teams suffer. Use Data Set 54a.

QS54b. Compute the regression line for predicting number of cars sold in a year from salesperson's years of experience. Use Data Set 54b.

EXCEL QUICKGUIDE 55

The Histogram Tool

What the Histogram Tool Does

The Histogram tool creates an image of the frequencies of set values organized in classes.

The Data Set

The data set used in this example is titled HISTOGRAM, and the question is, "What is the frequency of 1st-year, 2nd-year, 3rd-year, and 4th-year students in a sample of 25 students?"

Variable	Description
Class	1 = 1st year, 2 = 2nd year, 3 = 3rd year, and 4 = 4th year
Bin	The group assignment criteria (class = 1–4)

Using the Histogram Tool

1. Select the Data Analysis option from the Data tab.
2. Double-click the Histogram option in the Data Analysis dialog box, and you will see the Histogram dialog box shown in Figure 55.1.
3. Click the RefEdit button in the Input Range entry box and select the data you want to use in the analysis. In this example, it is Cells A1 through A26. Click the RefEdit button.
4. Click the RefEdit button in the Bin Range entry box and select the data you want to use in the analysis. In this example, it is Cells B1 through B5. Click the RefEdit button again.
5. Be sure to check the Labels box.
6. Click the Output Range button, click the RefEdit button, and enter the output range. In this example, Cell C1 is selected. Click the RefEdit button again.
7. Click the Cumulative Percentage and Chart Output boxes.
8. Click OK.

The Final Output

The results in Figure 55.2 show the frequency of each value in the Bin Range plus the cumulative frequency. A histogram of the frequencies and a line showing the cumulative frequencies are also produced.

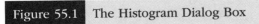

Figure 55.1 The Histogram Dialog Box

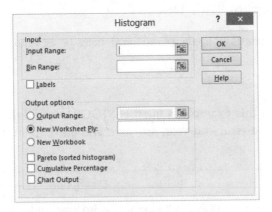

Figure 55.2 The Histogram Output

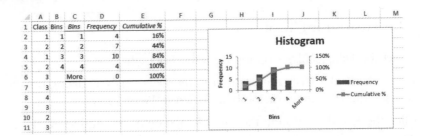

Check Your Understanding

To check your understanding of the Histogram tool, do the following two problems and check your answers in Figures A.29 and A.30 in Appendix A.

QS55a. Generate a histogram for choice of meal (1 = vegan, 2 = vegetarian, 3 = meat) for 100 diners. Use Data Set 55a.

QS55b. Generate a histogram for favorite type of recreation (1 = walking, 2 = running, 3 = swimming, 4 = yoga) for 200 community members. Use Data Set 55b.

Appendix A

Answers to QuickGuide Questions

QuickGuide		Answer
1	a	The average number of visitors is 5,071.
	b	The average age is 23.35 years.
2	a	The average test score is 77.25.
	b	The average number of seniors who received shingles vaccinations in five midwestern states is 337,588.
3	a	The median price of a home across the 10 communities is $324,544.
	b	The median height is 74.50 inches.
4	a	The mode or the preferred topping is 1, or hot fudge.
	b	The modal age range is 2, or between 21 and 34 years of age.
5	a	The two modes are 2 (female) and 3 (unspecified).
	b	The modes are 5, 4, 3, 2, and 1. Each neighborhood is equally represented.
6	a	The geometric mean for the average achievement score is 0.8105, or 81%.
	b	The geometric mean for the average monthly amount of groceries purchased is $529.68.
7	a	The standard deviation for the spelling test scores is 0.11.
	b	The standard deviation for the number of adults who received flu shots is 2,278.53.
8	a	The standard deviation for the number of users is 1,541.33.
	b	The standard deviation for sales is 2,351.10.
9	a	The variance for the sample of math test scores is 192.03.
	b	The variance for the aggressive behaviors scores is 8.12.

(Continued)

(Continued)

QuickGuide		Answer
10	a	The variance for annual income across the 25 cities is $300,445,168.
	b	The variance for the body mass index scores for the population of elementary school children is 5.55.
11	a	Here is the frequency distribution for the two levels of status: Level 1: 52 Level 2: 48
	b	Here is the frequency distribution for the three levels of rating: Level 1: 72 Level 2: 80 Level 3: 98
12	a	Here are the cumulative probabilities for sales by month:

Month	Sales	NORM.DIST
January	$25,456	6.81%
February	$25,465	6.81%
March	$44,645	25.61%
April	$54,345	40.78%
May	$55,456	42.67%
June	$56,456	44.38%
July	$65,456	59.88%
August	$66,787	62.10%
September	$76,564	76.84%
October	$87,656	88.81%
November	$98,465	95.42%
December	$94,657	93.59%
Sales mean	$59,704.64	
Sales SD	$22,979.48	

QuickGuide		Answer
	b	Here are the cumulative probabilities for number of cars in inventory by quarter:

Quarter	Number	NORM.DIST
First	234	19.55%
Second	245	22.94%
Third	346	63.00%
Fourth	434	89.74%
Quarter mean	$314.75	
Quarter SD	$94.13	

QuickGuide		Answer
13	a	The 50th percentile for use of library facilities is 123.
	b	The 80th percentile for number of meals prepared is 312.
14	a	The percentage rank for a raw score of 89 is 79%.
	b	The percentage rank for a house priced at $156,500 is 0%.
15	a	The value of the second quartile is 16.
	b	The value of the third quartile is $558,500.
16	a	A score of 57 is a rank of 41st.
	b	Team 6 ranked 14th.
17	a	Here are the standardized scores:

ID	Test Score	STANDARDIZE
1	75	−1.36
2	80	−0.75
3	85	−0.14
4	87	0.11
5	74	−1.49
6	96	1.21
7	95	1.09
8	73	−1.61
9	90	0.48

(Continued)

(Continued)

QuickGuide		Answer

ID	Test Score	STANDARDIZE
10	88	0.23
11	95	1.09
12	87	0.11
13	89	0.35
14	85	−0.14
15	84	−0.26
16	93	0.84
17	90	0.48
18	74	−1.49
19	77	−1.12
20	76	−1.24
21	96	1.21
22	86	−0.01
23	81	−0.63
24	98	1.46
25	99	1.58
AVERAGE	85.58	
STDEV.S	7.87	

QuickGuide		Answer
	b	The corresponding standardized score for a raw score of 76 is −1.11.
18	a	The covariance between first response and correct responses is 5.58.
	b	The covariance between study time and grade point average is −0.31.
19	a	The correlation between children retained and parental involvement is −.36.
	b	The correlation between the number of water plants and the incidence of disease is −.23.
20	a	The correlation between years in teaching and teaching evaluations from high school students is .15.
	b	The correlation between ice cream consumption and crime rate is .31.

QuickGuide		Answer
21	a	The intercept is 50,435.78.
	b	The intercept is 7.45.
22	a	The slope is 7,134.20.
	b	The slope is −0.04.
23	a	The trend for new income scores is as follows: $74,692.06 $63,990.76 $66,844.44 $70,411.54 $76,832.32
	b	The trend for new success scores is as follows: 7.2 7.3 6.9 7.2
24	a	The forecast for new losses is as follows: 4 losses 5 losses 10 losses 7 losses 8 losses
	b	The forecast for new American history test scores is as follows: 80 82 85
25	a	The squared correlation between height and weight is .4.
	b	The squared correlation between quality of care and decline in infant mortality is .8.
26	a	The value of CHISQ.DIST is 0.28.
	b	The value of CHISQ.DIST is 0.02.

(Continued)

(Continued)

QuickGuide		Answer
27	a	The probability is .75 that the proportions of actual and expected community center users differ.
	b	The probability is .06 that people have a preference for a particular type of detergent.
28	a	The F.DIST value is 0.96.
	b	The F.DIST value is 0.83.
29	a	The CONFIDENCE.NORM is 5,987.80.
	b	The CONFIDENCE.NORM is 4.78.
30	a	The F.TEST value is 0.12.
	b	The F.TEST value is 0.18.
31	a	The T.DIST value is 0.62.
	b	The T.DIST value is 0.97.
32	a	The probability associated with a t test for the difference between test scores 2.86×10^{-12}.
	b	The probability associated with a t test for the difference between ratings for two different dishes is 0.20.
33	a	The probability that a math test score of 83 is characteristic of the entire set of scores is .98.
	b	The probability that the free-throw shooting percentage of 63 is unique is .05.
34	a	The fifth smallest income is $207,066.
	b	The third smallest score is 86.
35	a	The ID numbers of the individuals with the 23rd highest score are 13, 30, 31, 34, 35, 63, and 80.
	b	The 10th largest value is 0.09.
36	a	The average sales value for those members of the A Team is $520,982.

QuickGuide		Answer
	b	The average incidence of infections (per 1,000 patients) in hospitals in communities with fewer than 200,000 people is 5.63.
37	a	The number of people who purchased insurance is 6.
	b	The numbers of people who gave their ages and years of service are 9 and 14.
38	a	The number of people who decided to enroll is 30.
	b	The number of communities that adopted curbside or alley recycling is 15.
39	a	The number of students from a group of 35 who did not show up in an elective class is 10.
	b	The number of communities that do not have adequate tax bases is 6.
40	a	The number of students who were admitted to the program and subsequently enrolled is 16.
	b	The number of businesses that are open on the weekend is 17.
41	a	(see spreadsheet below)

	A	B	C	D	E
1	City	Tax Rate		*Tax Rate*	
2	1	3.0%			
3	2	3.5%		Mean	0.057
4	3	6.0%		Standard Error	0.007
5	4	7.0%		Median	0.058
6	5	4.8%		Mode	0.07
7	6	6.7%		Standard Deviation	0.021
8	7	9.8%		Sample Variance	0.000
9	8	3.7%		Kurtosis	0.271
10	9	5.6%		Skewness	0.542
11	10	7.0%		Range	0.068
12				Minimum	0.030
13				Maximum	0.098
14				Sum	0.571
15				Count	10

Descriptive statistics for tax rate.

(Continued)

(Continued)

QuickGuide		Answer
	b	

b

	A	B	C	D	E
1	Week	Sales		Sales	
2	1	45			
3	2	41		Mean	49.75
4	3	47		Standard Error	5.56
5	4	66		Median	46
6				Mode	#N/A
7				Standard Deviation	11.12
8				Sample Variance	123.58
9				Kurtosis	3.12
10				Skewness	1.70
11				Range	25
12				Minimum	41
13				Maximum	66
14				Sum	199
15				Count	4

Descriptive statistics for sales.

42 a

	A	B	C
1	Number of Spaces Used		#N/A
2	80		#N/A
3	82		87.33
4	100		91.00
5	91		91.00
6	82		84.67
7	81		86.67
8	97		92.00
9	98		94.00
10	87		93.00
11	94		87.33

Moving average for number of spaces used.

b

	A	B	C	D
1	Weeks	Hours Training		MOVING AVERAGE
2	1	16		#N/A
3	2	19		19.00
4	3	19		17.50
5	4	16		16.00
6	5	16		17.00
7	6	18		16.50
8	7	15		15.00
9	8	15		16.00
10	9	17		17.00
11	10	17		16.50
12	11	16		17.50
13	12	19		19.00

Moving average for hours of training.

QuickGuide		Answer
43	a	

	A	B
	ID	RANDOM NUMBER
1		
2	1	-0.81621
3	2	0.420261
4	3	2.286207
5	4	1.433779
6	5	2.176827
7	6	-0.94767
8	7	1.735674
9	8	2.368135
10	9	-0.21546
11	10	1.994423
12	11	1.066258
13	12	2.064195
14	13	0.159425
15	14	0.016927

A set of 25 random numbers. The list of random numbers you generate will be different than what you see in Figure A5.

b

	A	B
2	1	0.858813
3	2	1.891785
4	3	-0.112464
5	4	1.379432
6	5	2.327903
7	6	1.119584
8	7	0.663471
9	8	0.115932
10	9	2.163025
11	10	2.147371

Random numbers associated with participants. The list of random numbers you generate will be different than what you see in Figure A5.

(Continued)

(Continued)

QuickGuide		Answer
44	a	

a.

▲	A	B	C	D	E
1	Salary	Point	Salary	Rank	Percent
2	$93,110	3	$97,935	1	100.00%
3	$88,794	9	$93,287	2	94.70%
4	$97,935	1	$93,110	3	89.40%
5	$81,601	17	$92,234	4	84.20%
6	$72,021	7	$91,416	5	78.90%
7	$83,162	2	$88,794	6	73.60%
8	$91,416	6	$83,162	7	68.40%
9	$55,987	20	$82,651	8	63.10%
10	$93,287	4	$81,601	9	57.80%
11	$57,681	12	$77,665	10	52.60%
12	$62,769	18	$77,108	11	47.30%
13	$77,665	5	$72,021	12	42.10%
14	$64,168	13	$64,168	13	36.80%
15	$57,915	16	$63,876	14	31.50%
16	$51,383	11	$62,769	15	26.30%
17	$63,876	14	$57,915	16	21.00%
18	$92,234	10	$57,681	17	15.70%
19	$77,108	19	$57,616	18	10.50%
20	$57,616	8	$55,987	19	5.20%
21	$82,651	15	$51,383	20	0.00%

Rank and percentile scores for salary.

b.

▲	A	B	C	D	E
1	Hours Studying	Point	Hours Studying	Rank	Percent
2	16	8	32	1	100.00%
3	21	14	31	2	92.80%
4	24	11	29	3	85.70%
5	25	15	28	4	78.50%
6	26	5	26	5	71.40%
7	12	4	25	6	64.20%
8	8	3	24	7	57.10%
9	32	13	22	8	50.00%
10	14	2	21	9	42.80%
11	17	10	17	10	35.70%
12	29	1	16	11	21.40%
13	16	12	16	11	21.40%
14	22	9	14	13	14.20%
15	31	6	12	14	7.10%
16	28	7	8	15	0.00%

Rank and percentile score for studying.

QuickGuide		Answer

45 a

▲	A	B	C	D	E	F	G	H	I	J	K	L
1	ID											Sample
2	148	104	69	78	149	85	143	131	98	67		67
3	96	123	144	119	51	140	135	122	57	104		59
4	101	133	59	122	149	50	106	67	93	68		124
5	53	131	104	147	69	80	96	101	89	67		85
6	51	73	85	59	114	145	142	126	133	55		122
7	99	118	133	63	140	96	125	128	109	134		89
8	109	67	85	56	122	93	144	67	111	86		68
9	79	87	106	124	88	119	96	67	146	82		73
10	112	114	117	111	66	99	50	149	119	84		133
11												112
12												78
13												140
14												134
15												131
16												96

A random selection of 15 participants.

b

▲	A	B	C	D	E	F	G	H	I	J	K	L
1	ID											Sample
2	148	104	69	78	149	85	143	131	98	67		104
3	96	123	144	119	51	140	135	122	57	104		119
4	101	133	59	122	149	50	106	67	93	68		89
5	53	131	104	147	69	80	96	101	89	67		101
6	51	73	85	59	114	145	142	126	133	55		145
7	99	118	133	63	140	96	125	128	109	134		59
8	109	67	85	56	122	93	144	67	111	86		85
9	79	87	106	124	88	119	96	67	146	82		87
10	112	114	117	111	66	99	50	149	119	84		123
11												79
12												96
13												67
14												51
15												93
16												55

A random selection of 20 scores.

46 a

▲	A	B	C	D	E	F	G
1		Homeowners 1	Homeowners 2		z-Test: Two Sample for Means		
2		3	4				
3		5	3			Homeowners 1	Homeowners 2
4		1	3		Mean	3.50	3.90
5		1	4		Known Variance	1.55	0.79
6		2	5		Observations	20	20
7		3	5		Hypothesized Mean Difference	0	
8		2	5		z	-1.17	
9		4	4		P(Z<=z) one-tail	0.12	
10		5	3		z Critical one-tail	1.64	
11		5	3		P(Z<=z) two-tail	0.24	
12		4	2		z Critical two-tail	1.96	
13		4	3		P(T<=t) two-tail	0.33	
14		3	4		t Critical two-tail	2.09	
15		3	5				
16		4	5				
17		4	4				
18		5	5				
19		4	4				
20		3	4				
21		5	3				
22							
23	VAR.P	1.55	0.79				

The z value of −1.17 indicates that there is no significant difference between groups of homeowners.

(Continued)

QuickGuide		Answer
	b	

b

	A	B	C	D	E	F	G	H
1		Group 1	Group 2		z-Test: Two Sample for Means			
2		139	96					
3		134	90			Group 1	Group 2	
4		125	113		Mean	121.36	110.86	
5		120	101		Known Variance	308.52	170.27	
6		115	104		Observations	14	14	
7		91	123		Hypothesized M	0		
8		129	106		z	1.80		
9		141	106		P(Z<=z) one-tail	0.04		
10		122	107		z Critical one-tai	1.64		
11		154	139		P(Z<=z) two-tail	0.07		
12		121	130		z Critical two-tai	1.96		
13		117	107					
14		94	106					
15		97	124					
16								
17	VAR.P	308.52	170.265					

The z value of 1.80 indicates that there is a significant difference between the two groups.

47

a

	A	B	C	D	E
1	Before Course	After Course	t-Test: Paired Two Sample for Means		
2	144	139			
3	144	145		Before Course	After Course
4	145	146	Mean	142.58	145.67
5	141	149	Variance	4.08	58.93
6	145	139	Observations	24	24
7	141	147	Pearson Correlation	-0.08	
8	142	143	Hypothesized Mean Difference	0.00	
9	143	166	df	23	
10	142	151	t Stat	-1.87	
11	145	144	P(T<=t) one-tail	0.04	
12	140	140	t Critical one-tail	1.71	
13	145	144	P(T<=t) two-tail	0.07	
14	140	136	t Critical two-tail	2.07	
15	141	140			
16	140	137			
17	142	149			
18	140	147			
19	140	167			
20	145	146			
21	144	145			
22	145	145			
23	144	137			
24	144	150			

The t value of −1.87 indicates that there is a significant difference between before and after scores.

QuickGuide		Answer

b

◢	A	B	C	D	E
1	BMI Before	BMI After	t-Test: Paired Two Sample for Means		
2	29	24			
3	25	26		*BMI Before*	*BMI After*
4	24	23	Mean	25.90	25.30
5	35	27	Variance	12.52	5.48
6	22	25	Observations	20	20
7	28	27	Pearson Correlation	0.50	
8	26	24	Hypothesized Mean Difference	0.00	
9	27	25	df	19	
10	26	24	t Stat	0.86	
11	23	22	P(T<=t) one-tail	0.20	
12	21	23	t Critical one-tail	1.73	
13	21	25	P(T<=t) two-tail	0.40	
14	24	23	t Critical two-tail	2.09	
15	25	25			
16	24	26			
17	32	30			
18	26	22			
19	30	28			
20	25	27			
21	25	30			

The *t* value of 0.86 indicates that the body mass index score did not change as a function of the treatment.

48   **a**

◢	A	B	C	D	E
1	Group 1	Group 2	t-Test: Two-Sample Assuming Unequal Variances		
2	9.8	6.5			
3	8.7	7.6		*Group 1*	*Group 2*
4	3.2	9.1	Mean	6.05	9.80
5	5.6	13.1	Variance	11.43	9.50
6	4.7	16.5	Observations	10	10
7	2	9.4	Hypothesized Mean Difference	0	
8	2.1	8	df	18	
9	6.6	9.8	t Stat	-2.59	
10	5.5	6.9	P(T<=t) one-tail	0.01	
11	12.3	11.1	t Critical one-tail	1.73	
12			P(T<=t) two-tail	0.02	
13			t Critical two-tail	2.10	
14					

The *t* value of −2.59 indicates that there is a significant difference between the two groups.

(Continued)

(Continued)

QuickGuide		Answer
	b	

b

	A	B	C	D	E
1	Public Debt	Private Debt	t-Test: Two-Sample Assuming Unequal Variances		
2	$ 13,267	$ 8,573			
3	$ 12,562	$ 10,150		Public Debt	Private Debt
4	$ 18,995	$ 10,607	Mean	$ 15,303.70	$ 10,607.50
5	$ 14,996	$ 10,531	Variance	$ 6,351,032.01	$ 30,830,306.27
6	$ 17,181	$ 7,572	Observations	10	14
7	$ 14,488	$ 7,103	Hypothesized Mean Difference	0	
8	$ 14,760	$ 8,497	df	19	
9	$ 18,591	$ 9,240	t Stat	2.79	
10	$ 16,704	$ 10,919	P(T<=t) one-tail	0.01	
11	$ 11,493	$ 9,770	t Critical one-tail	1.73	
12		$ 21,345	P(T<=t) two-tail	0.01	
13		$ 24,312	t Critical two-tail	2.09	
14		$ 5,463			
15		$ 4,423			

The *t* value of 2.79 indicates that there is a significant difference between the two groups.

49

a

	A	B	C	D	E	F
1	ID	Cessation	Control	t-Test: Two-Sample Assuming Equal Variances		
2	1	24	7			
3	2	21	12		Cessation	Control
4	3	23	14	Mean	33.00	22.74
5	4	24	15	Variance	168.33	152.76
6	5	32	21	Observations	19	19
7	6	45	33	Pooled Variance	160.55	
8	7	42	21	Hypothesized Mean Difference	0	
9	8	36	34	df	36	
10	9	52	32	t Stat	2.50	
11	10	12	3	P(T<=t) one-tail	0.01	
12	11	25	21	t Critical one-tail	1.69	
13	12	42	32	P(T<=t) two-tail	0.02	
14	13	57	43	t Critical two-tail	2.03	
15	14	43	23			
16	15	44	44			
17	16	23	23			
18	17	15	0			
19	18	44	31			
20	19	23	23			

The *t* value of 2.50 indicates that there is a significant difference between the cessation and control groups.

b

	A	B	C	D	E	F
1	ID	Bricks	Online	t-Test: Two-Sample Assuming Equal Variances		
2	1	$ 21,714	$ 21,992			
3	2	$ 20,309	$ 23,774		Bricks	Online
4	3	$ 22,819	$ 20,408	Mean	$ 24,429.92	$ 25,176.16
5	4	$ 21,370	$ 20,472	Variance	$ 9,931,818.91	$ 10,330,008.47
6	5	$ 25,595	$ 28,110	Observations	25	25
7	6	$ 23,995	$ 20,055	Pooled Variance	$ 10,130,913.69	
8	7	$ 29,876	$ 26,025	Hypothesized Mean Difference	0	
9	8	$ 27,677	$ 27,942	df	48	
10	9	$ 20,606	$ 24,014	t Stat	-0.83	
11	10	$ 28,850	$ 24,072	P(T<=t) one-tail	0.21	
12	11	$ 25,853	$ 29,150	t Critical one-tail	1.68	
13	12	$ 29,714	$ 21,294	P(T<=t) two-tail	0.41	
14	13	$ 20,537	$ 29,135	t Critical two-tail	2.01	
15	14	$ 28,800	$ 27,912			
16	15	$ 23,827	$ 21,160			
17	16	$ 24,379	$ 27,607			
18	17	$ 20,701	$ 24,776			
19	18	$ 23,803	$ 27,118			
20	19	$ 24,978	$ 28,089			
21	20	$ 21,522	$ 25,846			
22	21	$ 27,768	$ 29,369			
23	22	$ 22,363	$ 20,550			
24	23	$ 22,605	$ 26,375			
25	24	$ 22,603	$ 25,007			

The *t* value of −0.83 indicates there is no significant difference between the bricks-and-mortar and online programs.

QuickGuide		Answer

50 a

	A	B	C	D	E	F	G	H	I	J
1	Home School 1	Home School 2	Home School 3	Anova: Single Factor						
2	91	79	62							
3	72	81	100	SUMMARY						
4	97	86	67	Groups	Count	Sum	Average	variance		
5	84	86	92	Home School 1	25	1959	78.36	120.2		
6	67	90	94	Home School 2	25	2000	80	134.33		
7	78	70	82	Home School 3	25	2014	80.56	156.17		
8	82	60	83							
9	63	83	70							
10	73	90	89	ANOVA						
11	92	92	97	Source of Variation	SS	df	MS	F	-valu	F crit
12	66	78	70	Between Groups	65.36	2	32.68	0.24	0.79	3.12
13	76	94	60	Within Groups	9857.92	72	136.92			
14	66	64	61							
15	65	90	97	Total	9923.28	74				
16	86	83	78							

The *F* value of 0.24 indicates that there is no significant difference in math performance among the three groups, with Home School 3 having the highest average.

b

	A	B	C	D	E	F	G	H	I	J	K
1	Self Esteem 1	Self Esteem 2	Self Esteem 3	Self Esteem 4	Anova: Single Factor						
2	2	5	10	5							
3	1	3	8	4	SUMMARY						
4	5	3	9	2	Groups	Count	Sum	Average	Variance		
5	2	4	10	3	Self Esteem 1	20	61	3.05	2.79		
6	1	6	10	4	Self Esteem 2	20	101	5.05	2.26		
7	2	7	10	3	Self Esteem 3	20	182	9.1	0.62		
8	1	4	9	2	Self Esteem 4	20	62	3.1	1.57		
9	5	7	9	2							
10	1	6	10	5							
11	4	5	8	4	ANOVA						
12	2	5	9	4	Source of Variation	SS	df	MS	F	P-value	F crit
13	1	3	9	2	Between Groups	484.05	3	161.35	89.18	0.00	2.72
14	3	7	8	3	Within Groups	137.5	76	1.81			
15	3	7	9	5							
16	5	6	10	2	Total	621.55	79				
17	5	4	9	3							
18	5	5	8	1							
19	5	3	8	4							
20	3	4	10	1							
21	5	7	9	3							

The *F* value of 89.18 indicates that there is a significant difference among self-esteem programs, with Self-Esteem 3 having the highest average.

51 a

	A	B	C	D	E	F	G	H	I	J	K	L	M
1				Involvement			Anova: Two-Factor With Replication						
2			Level 1	Level 1	Level 2								
3		Males	78	84	88		SUMMARY	Level 1	Level 1	Level 2	Total		
4			70	76	76		Males						
5			79	79	76		Count	5	5	5	15		
6			65	78	99		Sum	355	397	421	1173		
7	Gender		63	80	82		Average	71	79.4	84.2	78.2		
8		Females	78	85	91		Variance	53.5	8.8	93.2	76.31		
9			63	79	82								
10			80	79	75		Females						
11			67	82	98		Count	5	5	5	15		
12			65	77	70		Sum	353	402	416	1171		
13							Average	70.60	80.40	83.20	78.07		
14							Variance	61.30	9.80	130.70	88.92		
15													
16							Total						
17							Count	10	10	10			
18							Sum	708	799	837			
19							Average	70.8	79.9	83.7			
20							Variance	51.07	8.54	99.79			
23							ANOVA						
24							Source of Variation	SS	df	MS	F	P-value	F crit
25							Sample	0.13	1	0.13	0.00	0.96	4.26
26							Columns	878.87	2	439.43	7.88	0.00	3.40
27							Interaction	5.27	2	2.63	0.04	0.96	3.40
28							Within	1429.2	24	59.55			
30							Total	2313.47	29				

The *F* values show no main effect for gender and no interaction effect, but a significant effect for level.

(Continued)

QuickGuide		Answer
	b	

	A	B	C	D	E	F	G	H	I	J	K
1			Teaching		Anova: Two-Factor With Replication						
2			In School	In Home							
3		High	3	6	SUMMARY	In School	In Home	Total			
4			6	5	High						
5			5	4	Count	5	5	10			
6			4	4	Sum	24	24	48			
7	Participation		6	5	Average	4.8	4.8	4.8			
8		Low	6	6	Variance	1.7	0.7	1.066666667			
9			5	7							
10			4	7	Low						
11			6	6	Count	5	5	10			
12			6	7	Sum	27	33	60			
13					Average	5.4	6.6	6			
14					Variance	0.8	0.3	0.89			
15											
16					Total						
17					Count	10	10				
18					Sum	51	57				
19					Average	5.1	5.7				
20					Variance	1.21	1.34				
21											
22											
23					ANOVA						
24					Source of Variation	SS	df	MS	F	P-value	F crit
25					Sample	7.20	1	7.20	8.23	0.01	4.49
26					Columns	1.80	1	1.80	2.06	0.17	4.49
27					Interaction	1.80	1	1.80	2.06	0.17	4.49
28					Within	14.00	16	0.88			
29											
30					Total	24.80	19				

The F values show a main effect for participation but no main effect for teaching or an interaction effect.

---

52   a

ANOVA						
Source of Variation	SS	df	MS	F	P-value	F crit
Rows	91.66	29	3.16	1.22	0.26	1.66
Columns	60.09	2	30.04	11.57	0.00	3.16
Error	150.58	58	2.60			
Total	302.32	89				

The F values show no main effect for experience, but a significant main effect for type of speaking program.

---

b

ANOVA						
Source of Variation	SS	df	MS	F	P-value	F crit
Rows	6049.10	19	318.37	1.11	0.41	2.17
Columns	102.40	1	102.40	0.36	0.56	4.38
Error	5451.60	19	286.93			
Total	11603.10	39				

The F values show neither a significant main effect for community or advertising rates.

QuickGuide		Answer
53	a	

	A	B	C		D	E	F
1	Community	Crime Rate	Ice Cream Conpsumption			*Crime Rate*	*Ice Cream Conpsumption*
2	A	8		36	Crime Rate	1	
3	B	4		22	Ice Cream Conpsumption	0.22	1
4	C	18		26			
5	D	15		44			
6	E	12		26			
7	F	17		21			
8	G	15		43			
9	H	33		43			
10	I	26		23			
11	J	12		24			
12	K	24		22			
13	L	56		49			
14	M	55		28			
15	N	43		19			
16	O	18		27			

The correlation between consumption of ice cream and crime rate is .22.

| | | b | |

	A	B	C	D	E
1	Speed	Accuracy		*Speed*	*Accuracy*
2	7	2	Speed	1	
3	5	3	Accuracy	-0.76	1
4	6	2			
5	7	3			
6	1	7			
7	1	7			
8	3	9			
9	2	2			
10	3	4			
11	4	7			
12	2	7			
13	8	1			
14	7	2			
15	1	8			
16	2	9			

The correlation between speed and accuracy is −.76.

| | | 54 | a | |

	A	B	C	D	E	F	G	H	I	J	K
1	Wins	Injuries	SUMMARY OUTPUT								
2	77	31									
3	67	34	*Regression Statistics*								
4	87	51	Multiple R	0.208626945							
5	98	54	R Square	0.043525202							
6	46	44	Adjusted R Square	-0.076034148							
7	76	35	Standard Error	20.10725981							
8	56	65	Observations	10							
9	78	71									
10	74	33	ANOVA								
11	33	64		df	SS	MS	F	*Significance F*			
12			Regression	1	147.18	147.18	0.36	0.56			
13			Residual	8	3234.42	404.30					
14			Total	9	3381.60						
15											
16				*Coefficients*	*Standard Error*	*t Stat*	*P-value*	*Lower 95%*	*Upper 95%*	*Lower 95.0%*	*Upper 95.0%*
17			Intercept	82.23	22.51	3.65	0.01	30.31	134.15	30.31	134.15
18			Injuries	-0.27	0.45	-0.60	0.56	-1.30	0.76	-1.30	0.76

The regression line is $Y' = -0.27X + 82.23$.

(Continued)

(Continued)

QuickGuide		Answer
	b	

b (Regression output table)

	A	B	C	D	E	F	G	H	I	J	K
1	Sales	Experience	SUMMARY OUTPUT								
2	120	12									
3	143	14	*Regression Statistics*								
4	100	8	Multiple R	0.662512151							
5	214	21	R Square	0.43892235							
6	165	15	Adjusted R Square	0.368787643							
7	242	16	Standard Error	46.34177137							
8	210	6	Observations	10							
9	222	12									
10	276	33	ANOVA								
11	243	31		df	SS	MS	F	Significance F			
12			Regression	1	13440.02181	13440.02181	6.258276009	0.036846916			
13			Residual	8	17180.47819	2147.559774					
14			Total	9	30620.5						
15											
16				Coefficients	Standard Error	t Stat	P-value	Lower 95%	Upper 95%	Lower 95.0%	Upper 95.0%
17			Intercept	121.59	32.26	3.77	0.01	47.19	195.99	47.19	195.99
18			Experience	4.28	1.71	2.50	0.04	0.33	8.23	0.33	8.23

The regression line is $Y' = 4.28X + 121.59$.

55

a

	A	B	C	D	E
1	Class	Bins	Bins	Frequency	Cumulative %
2	2	1	1	32	32%
3	2	2	2	34	66%
4	2	3	3	34	100%
5	3		More	0	100%
6	2				
7	3				
8	1				
9	1				
10	1				
11	3				

A histogram of meal choice by 100 diners.

---

b

	A	B	C	D	E
1	Class	Bins	Bins	Frequency	Cumulative %
2	3	1	1	52	26%
3	4	2	2	52	52%
4	1	3	3	48	76%
5	2	4	4	48	100%
6	4		More	0	100%
7	1				
8	2				
9	4				
10	4				
11	4				

A histogram of activity choice by 200 community members.

Appendix B

Using the Macintosh Excel Formula Builder

For Macintosh users, Excel offers a simple and direct way of using formulas called the Formula Builder. It allows the user to easily enter cell references and return values and can be used to create a formula or enter a specific function.

For example, in Figure B.1, there is a set of 10 scores. Here are the steps to use the AVERAGE function, the value of which will be returned to Cell B2.

Figure B.1	A Set of 10 Scores to Be Averaged

	A	B
1	7	
2	6	
3	8	
4	5	
5	6	
6	7	
7	8	
8	7	
9	6	
10	7	
11	AVERAGE	

1. Click the cell where you want the function to appear. In this example, it is Cell B2.

2. Select Insert → Function, and the Formula Builder Window will appear, as you see in Figure B.2.

Figure B.2   The Formula Builder Window

3. You can either search for the AVERAGE function using the search box or scroll down the list to find it. In either case, once you find the function you are looking for, double-click on it to produce the function arguments you see at the bottom of the Formula Builder window, as you see in Figure B.3.

Figure B.3   Specifying the AVERAGE Function in the Formula Builder

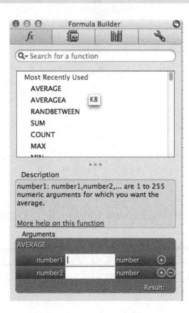

4. Enter the range of values you want to include in the number1 text box. You can enter additional ranges by clicking on the + sign and entering additional cell addresses. In this case, the range for the variable is A1:A10. Press the Enter key, and the value of the function appears, as shown in Figure B.4.

| Figure B.4 | The AVERAGE Function Returning the Average of a Set of 10 Scores |

Index